# THE CORRESPONDENCE (394-419)
# BETWEEN JEROME AND AUGUSTINE OF HIPPO

Carolinne White

Studies in Bible and Early Christianity
Volume 23

The Edwin Mellen Press
Lewiston/Queenston/Lampeter

**Library of Congress Cataloging in Publication Data**

This volume has been registered with The Library of Congress.

This is volume 23 in the continuing series
Studies in the Bible and Early Christianity
Volume 23 ISBN 0-88946-599-1
SBEC Series ISBN 0-88946-913-X

A CIP catalog record for this book
is available from the British Library.

Copyright © 1990  The Edwin Mellen Press

The Edwin Mellen Press
Box 450
Lewiston, New York
USA  14092

The Edwin Mellen Press
Box 67
Queenston, Ontario
CANADA  L0S 1L0

The Edwin Mellen Press, Ltd.
Lampeter, Dyfed, Wales
UNITED KINGDOM  SA48 7DY

Printed in the United States of America

# THE CORRESPONDENCE (394-419)
# BETWEEN JEROME AND AUGUSTINE OF HIPPO

# CONTENTS

## THE CORRESPONDENCE OF JEROME AND AUGUSTINE

# PREFACE

In an age of telecommunications when we take for granted instant access to friends or business colleagues the world over, it is sobering to come into close contact with a correspondence dating from a time when the difficulties of international communication were so great that letters were often delayed so long for various reasons that people had sometimes to wait for years for a response. In the face of such problems, Jerome and Augustine managed to continue a correspondence between the Holy Land and N.Africa on and off for twenty five years, gradually developing a respectful friendship and mutual loyalty in the cause of Christian orthodoxy. Their correspondence deals with important questions on theological and philosophical matters and with problems of friendship and is particularly valuable in that most of the letters from both parties are extant, giving us an insight into the ideas and attitudes of both these great men.

I am grateful to Andrew Louth for introducing me to Jerome and Augustine's world, to Hagith Sivan for advice and encouragement and to my husband Hugh for his constant support even during periods of domestic chaos.

# INTRODUCTION

The correspondence which Jerome in Bethlehem and Augustine in the north African town of Hippo maintained for a quarter of a century has been called 'a unique document in the early Church' and it is evident that it has been of particular interest to readers over the centuries; Peter the Venerable, for example, writing to the head of the Carthusians in the twelfth century, asks specifically to be sent a manuscript of Augustine's letters containing at the beginning the correspondence of Jerome and Augustine, as most of Peter's own copy has apparently been eaten by a bear![1] The correspondence is perhaps best known for the dispute generated by Augustine's queries and cricitisms of Jerome's work, a dispute which caused Jerome to display much fury and sarcasm and Augustine great tact and determination in his desire to establish friendly relations with this man and to enlist his help in grappling with a number of Scriptural problems. It is true that this dispute scarred their relations deeply, but there is more to the correspondence than this. As a whole, the seventeen extant letters which they addressed to one another between 394[2] and 419 A.D., a period of great intellectual ferment and social change during which Christianity became the official religion of the Empire although paganism was not yet dead, reveal much about the scholarly views, as well as the characters of these two outstanding men, 'les dernières gloires geminées d'un âge jusqu'ici insurpassé'.[3] Despite the broad similarities which drew them together - their familiarity with Classical culture and their devotion to the Christian Church - these two men, originating from opposite ends of the Latin-speaking Roman Empire, differed radically from each other in their temperament and interests and hence in their attitudes to points of mutual concern. Jerome, the elder of the two, after spending several years both in Rome and in the harsh desert of Chalcis, had retired to the Holy Land in 386 to devote himself to his work on the Bible and its exegesis - textual revision, translation and commentaries. His interests were primarily literary and philological rather than philosophical. Like Augustine, he was living in a monastic community; here at Bethlehem he was surrounded by admirers such as Paula and Eustochium and by a constant stream of visitors to the Holy Land, (though it seems that some of these were driven away by Jerome's quarrelsome disposition).[4] Augustine's monastic community, on the other hand, was situated in a thriving town of which he was to become bishop in 395; he, too, was supported by personal friends, a number of whom had known him since his youth and who had accompanied him from Italy, sharing his purpose. For Augustine had also spent some time at Rome - indeed, it seems that he and Jerome were both there in 383 although they apparently did not meet for they were moving in different circles,[5] and in fact they were never to meet - before his conversion at Milan to a life dedicated to Christ. This life was to involve him deeply in Church politics and controversy as an ecclesiastical administrator and in the fight against various heresies which would inspire many of his writings, aimed at setting forth true Christian doctrine.

But when Augustine first addressed a letter (Ep. 28) to Jerome he had not yet been made a bishop but was a mere priest, working from the community of like-minded men at Hippo, to which he had moved from Thagaste in 391. This letter starts as a letter of recommendation but also contains a request for Jerome to translate more works of the Greek exegetes, particularly Origen, to produce a translation of the Old Testament from the Septuagint of Origen's Hexapla rather than from the Hebrew and the question of the interpretation of a passage from Galatians. He appears to have decided to write to Jerome both because he had heard of this man's admirable asceticism and ambitious scholarly projects from his closest friend Alypius who had visited the Holy Land, and Jerome at Bethlehem, in 393, and was therefore eager to contact him and discuss with him issues of common interest, and more specifically, because he had recently read a copy of Jerome's commentary on Paul's Epistle to the Galatians (written in 388) in which he found that Jerome had given an unsatisfactory, even dangerous, interpretation of Gal. 2.11-14. It was his disagreement on this point in particular which was to lead to the famous controversy, prolonged because their letters were often lost or delayed and because of Jerome's refusal to reply to the question at issue; the discussion of the critical passage of Galatians is restricted to Ep. 28 (which never reached Jerome), Ep. 40 (largely a repetition of Ep. 28), Jerome's lengthy Ep. 112 and Augustine's final answer in his Ep. 82 - the other letters written while the dispute raged are largely devoted to expressions of love and respect or indignation and to the question of the extent to which criticism is permissible between Christian friends.

Cole-Turner[6] has shown that Augustine's Ep. 28 was written at the same period as his <u>Expositio Epistolae ad Galatas</u> and the short work <u>De Mendacio</u>, in which he discusses this Pauline passage, for it was an important text for Augustine at this time in his debates against the heretical views of Scripture held by the Manichees and Donatists. In writing to Jerome and expressing his disagreement with Jerome's interpretation, Augustine was trying to convince him of the validity of his own view and to gain his support for it against the heretics who were undermining the authority of the Bible, but his criticisms and questions are expressed in a polite and respectful, if firm manner, without the provocative or aggressive tone which Peter Brown appears to find in them.[7]

Unfortunately, due to the various accidents which befell their letters and to Jerome's reluctance to argue his point of view, Augustine had to wait ten years for a satisfactory reply (Jerome's Ep. 112) to his questions about the Galatians passage, during which time he was treated to a heavy dose of irony and abuse from Jerome, who felt that he was being attacked by a young upstart, (of course, Jerome's view of Augustine at this early stage of his career would have been startlingly different from the perspective we have on his achievement. Even Jerome came to have more respect for him - in 410, for example, he writes of Augustine to a mutual acquaintance as 'a holy man and learned bishop'), tainted by his involvement with the Manichees, whose main aim was to spread vicious lies about Jerome's doctrinal position. (Jerome might have suspected that Augustine was questioning his orthodoxy by his criticisms of Jerome's interpretation of Galatians, by his request that Jerome make it clear

which authors in his <u>De Viris Illustribus</u> were
heretical, and by questioning Jerome's motives in
translating the Old Testament from the Hebrew and
apparently disregarding the authority of the
Septuagint.) The deterioration of Jerome's relations
with his old friend Rufinus at this time, and the
subsequent violent rupture of their friendship against
the background of the Origenist controversy,[8] clearly
made Jerome suspicious of everybody, especially of
those who appeared to be hostile, although it is true
that he is more restrained in his invective against
Augustine than against many other apparent and real
opponents. It is possible that the break with Rufinus
made Jerome unwilling to enter a full-scale quarrel
with Augustine: this may explain his reluctance to
reply at any length to Augustine's first letters. In
questioning, and even criticising the older man's
position, Augustine, on the other hand, may well have
seen himself as the courageous younger man, likening
himself to Paul in the relevant Galatians passage who
dares to correct his elder (Jerome/Peter) who, he
feels, ought to accept the rebuke with humility;[9] but
humility was not one of Jerome's virtues and it took
some tactful writing on the part of Augustine before
Jerome grudgingly accepted that his correspondent was
more concerned with truth than abuse and their
relations could continue on a more friendly basis.
However, it is interesting to note that in his view of
their controversy, Erasmus supported Jerome, for whom
he had greater admiration, rather than Augustine, whom
he regarded as motivated by jealousy of Jerome, as well
as inferior to Jerome in everything but his rank as
bishop.[10]

Meanwhile, Jerome was also able to use broad hints

and veiled threats to frighten his opponent into
submission. While avoiding a full-scale reply to the
questions and criticisms he had read in Augustine's Ep.
40 and Ep. 67, Jerome did deign to send a brief and
very angry answer to his correspondent in 402 which
informed Augustine that Jerome had at last received
authenticated copies of his Ep. 28 and Ep. 40, as well
as Ep. 67; together with Ep. 102 Jerome sent a copy of
his Apology against Rufinus, possibly intending it as a
covert warning of what might happen if Augustine
continued to provoke him by attacking him publicly, as
Jerome believed he had done in Ep. 28 which was read by
people at Rome before it reached Jerome: here
Augustine could see how Jerome treated those friends
who betrayed or attacked him, as he felt Rufinus had
done. And in fact Augustine saw the threat clearly.
The rift between Jerome and Rufinus did genuinely
distress him,[11] but he also regarded it as it
affected his own friendship with Jerome; in Ep. 73 and
Ep. 82 he hints at parallels between the two
relationships, in the hope of warding off a similar
catastrophe by means of a timely reminder to Jerome of
the damage which his suspiciousness and over-
sensitivity to criticism could cause - this is what
Augustine regarded as the main reason for the problems
besetting their relations thus far.

When Augustine received Jerome's Ep. 102 and
realised how angry Jerome was and how the
misunderstandings between them had arisen, he wrote
back in a conciliatory tone with Ep. 73 - and this was
even before he had received Jerome's Ep. 105, which is,
if possible, even more bitter and provocative than Ep.
102. Augustine's Ep. 73 is largely concerned with the
question of how far friends should be able to go in

their criticism of each other and the spirit in which they should take criticism, rather than with doctrinal or Scriptural problems, for at this point the state of their developing friendship had become the main issue. It seems that this letter did succeed in pacifying Jerome, for his short Ep. 115, written after the receipt of Ep. 73, is far gentler and more respectful in tone than either Ep. 102 or Ep. 105.

But even before he received this, Jerome had felt able at last, once Augustine's Ep. 67 and Ep. 71 had clarified the situation while still urging a reply to the criticisms of Ep. 28 and Ep. 40, to write a lengthy defence of his interpretation of the Galatians passage. It was in reply to this that Augustine wrote his Ep. 82, probably in 405, which brought this controversy to a close, with both men apparently holding firmly to their original views.

It seems that after the more or less steady flow of letters during the years 402-405 (even though their letters often crossed), a pause in their correspondence now followed, as if both men were exhausted by the problems so far involved in their relations with one another and were hesitant to instigate any discussion which might meet similar difficulties. However, in 411 Jerome addressed a letter to Marcellinus and Anapsychia in which he praises Augustine and advises them to consult him on the question of the origin of human souls. This may be why Augustine in 415 addressed a letter, or rather a short treatise, to Jerome in which he discusses four possible theories of the soul's origin and implies that he broadly agrees with Jerome[12] that the most attractive theory is that God creates each soul for each individual at birth or conception i.e. the so-called creationist view. Ep.

166, the longest of Augustine's letters, was written at a time when both Jerome and Augustine were becoming increasingly involved in the Pelagian controversy, which had its focus first in North Africa while Pelagius was living there, and then in Palestine where Pelagius moved in about 410.[13] This was a cause on which they could agree and which was to inspire much passion in them both for the rest of their lives (Jerome died in 419 or 420, his last work being his Dialogue against the Pelagians, while Augustine lived on till 430 and had to spend his extreme old age combatting Pelagius' ideas as defended by Bishop Julian of Eclanum.[14]

By 415 it was becoming clear that Pelagius' views were not only dangerous but also increasing in popularity - indeed, his ideas were in some ways very attractive and hard to refute. The issues discussed by Augustine in Ep. 166 must have been highlighted by the Pelagian controversy and particularly by Pelagius' view of original sin and Augustine felt a desperate need to reach a clear position on the problems involved so that he could take a firm stand against Pelagius and his supporters. But although Jerome also felt strongly that Pelagius had to be condemned and although he had a definite personal involvement in the matter,[15] he treated Augustine's pleas for enlightenment in the same way as he had treated many of Augustine's earlier letters - by avoiding to reply. It is unlikely that he could have taken offence this time for Augustine's letter is a model of deference - Augustine shows that he had learned some lessons from the Galatians controversy and that he knows Jerome must be handled with care. More probable is it that Jerome had no clear answers to Augustine's problems; after all, if

Augustine was unable to sort out the contradictions involved in holding the creationist view of the soul side by side with a firm belief in original sin and to come down in favour of any other view of the soul's origin, it is hardly likely that Jerome would be capable of providing a convincing explanation.

This failure to reply directly also applies to Augustine's Ep. 167, sent to Jerome (like Ep. 166) in Orosius' hands in the same year and also probably inspired by the challenge of Pelagius' views on sin. In it Augustine asks Jerome for his advice on the interpretation of James 2.10. with its implication that all sins are equally serious. In what way is this true? But Jerome cannot help and it is only in the brief Ep. 134, written in 416 after the receipt of Ep. 166 and Ep. 167 but without engaging with their contents, that Jerome refers to one of Augustine's requests: in Ep. 82, written some eleven years earlier, Augustine had asked him for a copy of his complete translation of the Old Testament from Origen's Hexapla version which Jerome had mentioned. In fact it is unclear whether a complete translation ever existed; it is only known that Jerome translated the Psalter, Job, Chronicles, Proverbs, Ecclesiastes and the Song of Songs from the Septuagint (and now only his version of Job and the prefaces to his translations of Chronicles and the Song of Songs are extant). It is possible that Jerome only completed these before turning to a new translation direct from the Hebrew, but if so he is characteristically unwilling to admit that his claims for its completeness were illegitimate and in Ep. 134 he pretends that it has been lost - due to 'someone's dishonesty', he says enigmatically. If Jerome is lying here in order to cover up a previous lie, it is hardly

surprising that his interpretation of Gal. 2.11-14
involved the explanation that Paul was dishonest when
he rebuked Peter and that Peter was only pretending to
side with the extremists among the Jewish Christians!

The last three extant letters are all from Jerome -
brief letters probably written in the last year or two
of his life, for their correspondence was at last cut
short by Jerome's death. These final letters seem also
to relate to the culmination of the struggle against
Pelagius, though their brevity and enigmatic quality do
not permit us to learn much about the relations between
Jerome and Augustine at this time. It is probable that
there were more letters between them from this period
which are now lost.[16] Certainly they appear united
in their hatred of Pelagius and as victims of Pelagius'
hatred - in fact, Jerome's monastery at Bethlehem was
attacked by supporters of Pelagius in 416 and Jerome
almost lost his life. In Ep. 141 and Ep. 143 Jerome
congratulates Augustine warmly on his successes against
the heretics, in particular against Pelagius' follower
Caelestius. If Jerome remained in disagreement with
Augustine about certain issues such as the
infallibility of the Septuagint, their correspondence
did at least end with both men respecting and admiring
one another for his work and united, despite their
difficulties, in their devotion to the Catholic church.

1. Brown p. 274; cf. Lietzmann p. 374 who says that
the letters belong 'zu den wertvollsten Dokumente der
Geschichte'; Peter the Venerable Ep. 24 (ed. Giles
Constable, Cambridge, Mass. 1967).

2. Brown p. 74 wrongly states that Augustine first addressed a letter to Jerome in 392.

3. Simard p. 38.

4. Cf. Hunt p. 179.

5. In 383-4 Augustine was teaching at Rome and still involved with the Manichees, while Jerome was moving in the top Christian circles, engaged in work on the Bible at the instigation of Pope Damasus and in promoting asceticism; cf. Aug. Conf. V.8.14-12.22 [CCL 27.64-70], Simard p. 16.

6. R. Cole-Turner in AugStud 11 (1980) 155-166.

7. Brown pp. 274-5.

8. See Lardet's edition of the Apology against Rufinus for an account of the Origenist controversy.

9. Cf. Moehler p. 18.

10. See Erasmi Opuscula ed. J. Ferguson (The Hague 1933) p. 167.

11. In his Ep. 73.6 Augustine writes,'I was very upset that such terrible discord should have arisen between two such dear and intimate people...' Cf. Aug. Ep. 82.1.

12. For a contrary but unconvincing interpretation see O'Connell p. 11.

13. It appears that before his move to Palestine Pelagius met Augustine at Carthage and that he later met Jerome at Bethlehem.

14. Cf. Brown ch. 32.

15. Pelagius seems to have been an old rival of his - in fact, they may have known each other at Rome and soon Pelagius was definitely an unwelcome presence in the Holy Land, disturbing Jerome's peace.

16. In his Ep. 143 Jerome refers to two letters, one from Augustine and Alypius and one from himself which are now unknown.

# FRIENDSHIP BY CORRESPONDENCE

As Jerome and Augustine never met, they had to rely on
letters, and on the verbal messages of mutual friends,
for the communication by which their friendship
remained dynamic. This was not so uncommon at this
period, when the Christian Church had become a vast
network of interrelating communities throughout the
Roman Empire, when travel was difficult and time-
consuming, but when communication between those who
were passionately committed to the survival of the
Church and the struggle against heresy was felt to be
of vital importance for the exchange of news, mutual
encouragement, spiritual inspiration, discussions of
questions of dogma and for maintaining a sense of
community. As the Church expanded and assumed an
increasing amount of responsibility in society and as
the problems against which it had to struggle became
more numerous and more clearly defined, so the number
of letters written by Christians increased.
Furthermore, the cosmopolitan atmosphere at this time
was also conducive to the formation of friendships all
over the Empire, with people often making friends while
away at university in Athens, Alexandria or Rome,
friendships which they managed to maintain for many
years after their student days, usually by means of
letters. Many of the leading figures of the day formed
friendly relations with one another, thereby spreading
a whole network of friendships throughout the Empire,
from Ambrose in Milan to Basil in Cappadocia, from
Paulinus in Nola to Augustine in Hippo and Jerome in
Bethlehem. And did not John Cassian meet John
Chrysostom in Constantinople before moving to the West,

Augustine meet Ambrose in Milan before returning to N. Africa and Jerome meet Pammachius in Rome and Gregory of Nazianzus in Constantinople before retiring to Bethlehem?

However, despite the great dependence of such friends and of the Christian Church as a whole on correspondence, maintaining relations by means of letters could be problematic. Augustine complains that letters are in many ways unsatisfactory, for they often take a long time - sometimes even several years - to reach their destination, it is hard to find reliable messengers and there is the danger that they will be lost or at least will cross in the post. Although letters are usually seen as a satisfactory substitute for personal contact, Augustine in particular sometimes voices his disappointment and frustration with this means of communication and his longing for his friend's physical presence;[1] these must have been feelings he experienced particularly in his correspondence with Jerome in which there were so many false starts and misunderstandings and from whom he was separated by a distance of 2000km.

But at their best, letters could keep friends in each other's thoughts, could enable people to get to know each other even without meeting[2] and provide a substitute for conversation; both Jerome and Augustine, echoing Cicero,[3] speak of a friend as someone with whom you can talk as to a second self, and this includes those friends whom they never actually met but with whom they maintained a friendship by correspondence. For even though so many of these letters were written by high-profile Christians and often centred on difficult theological or ecclesiastical issues, few are completely devoid of any

personal element. This is certainly true of the
correspondence between Jerome and Augustine, for
although their letters are full of discussions which
would interest most Christians - and indeed were often
intended to be read by others - they are nevertheless
private letters, written with a particular addressee in
mind and with the underlying but important intention of
fostering a loving relationship in Christ. Their
content might make them fit into the category of
Moralbrief,[4] but this does not mean that each letter
is merely a one-way lecture; as a whole, their
correspondence with one another offers a fascinating
combination of literary, personal and official
elements.

Jerome and Augustine shared a belief in the
possibility - and for Augustine, the importance - of
spiritual friendships between Christians and indeed the
two of them offered promising material for such a
relationship since both of them were dedicated
Christians, sharing many of the same concerns and a
high degree of intellectuality. However, their widely
divergent characters were reflected in their attitudes
to friendship and the different emphasis they put on
the various traditional ideals of true friendship which
they had inherited from ancient philosophy and popular
thought and which they were now adapting to a Christian
context. Friendship was important to Augustine
throughout his life and his thoughts about it
influenced much of his theological, monastic and
ecclesiological thinking. He came to believe strongly
in the stability of human relationships founded on a
shared devotion to God - this was one reason why he was
so shocked by the rift between Jerome and Rufinus; the
Spirit of Christ should form a profound unity, not only

between two close friends but throughout the Church. This unity and harmony, he believed, could survive criticism and rebuke from one's friend; rebuke is healthy and indeed it is the most important obligation of friendship,[5] for no one can be a true friend unless he is first a friend of truth.[6] But while Augustine firmly rejects the idea, expressed in antiquity, that openness and honesty were detrimental to friendships, Jerome, who in general had a more ambivalent attitude to friendship than Augustine, stresses rather that friendship should be based on an uncritical loyalty and should be free from suspicion, anger and bitterness (which he seems to believe are the necessary accompaniments to criticism). This is not a state which Jerome found easy to achieve, being by nature distrustful. He had more sympathy for the ancient adage which stated that loyalty, or trustworthiness, were rarely to be found.[7] It is not only in his letters to Augustine that Jerome's suspiciousness and sensitivity to criticism are evident, but in these he does give utterance, in reaction to Augustine's ideas, to some of his own thoughts about the nature of Christian friendship and from them it becomes clear how far his negative feelings obstructed the course of their correspondence and their friendship, even though their last letters to each other are devoid of acrimony and characterised by a kind of friendly, if slightly cautious respect, indicating that they had perhaps reached a compromise on the question of how their friendship should be conducted.

1. Aug. Ep. 28.1.

2. This is connected with the idea, found in Christian and non-Christian writings, that a letter could be an image of the soul or a mirror of the mind, reflecting a man's inner self. Cf. Basil Ep. 163 [ed. Courtonne (Paris 1961) II.96] and Paulinus of Nola Ep. 13.2 to Pammachius, Jerome's friend [CSEL 29.85].

3. Cicero Laelius (De Amicitia) 21.80.

4. According to H. Peter pp. 225-242.

5. Cf. Aug. dCD 1.25, 3.22 [CCL 47.26, 90-91].

6. Cf. Aug. Ep. 155.1 to Macedonius.

7. 'Rara est in hominibus fides' (Phaedrus Fab. III.9.1); cf. Jer. Comm. in Micah 7.5 [CCL 76.507-510].

# CHRONOLOGY OF CORRESPONDENCE

The problems relating to the chronology of the correspondence derive from the fact that there are apparently some letters missing to which Jerome and Augustine refer (and there may be others which have been lost but of which we have no record), that their letters were often delayed or went astray and that for some letters we have no way of dating them accurately but can only rely on guesswork and probability.

It seems that their letters were not assembled into complete collections but into various groups, as in the early MSS.

The order and dating of the extant letters which we have accepted for this edition are as follows:

| AUTHOR DATE | LETTER NO. | CSEL VOL.NO.and PAGE | |
|---|---|---|---|
| Augustine 394/5 | Ep. 28(Jer. 56) | 34.1 | pp.103-113 |
| Jerome 397 | Ep. 103(Aug. 39) | 55 | pp.237-238 |
| Augustine 399 | Ep. 40(Jer. 67) | 34.2 | pp.69-81 |
| Augustine 402 | Ep. 67(Jer. 101) | 34.2 | pp.237-239 |
| Jerome 402 | Ep. 102(Aug. 68) | 55 | pp.234-236 |
| Augustine 403 | Ep. 71(Jer. 104) | 34.2 | pp.248-255 |

18

| | | | |
|---|---|---|---|
| Jerome 403/4 | Ep. 105(Aug. 72) | 55 | pp.242-246 |
| Augustine 404 | Ep. 73(Jer. 110) | 34.2 | pp.263-278 |
| Jerome 404 | Ep. 112(Aug. 75) | 55 | pp.367-393 |
| Jerome 404-405 | Ep. 115(Aug. 81) | 55 | pp.396-397 |
| Augustine 404-405 | Ep. 82(Jer. 116) | 34.2 | pp.351-387 |
| Augustine 415 | Ep. 166(Jer. 131) | 44 | pp.545-585 |
| Augustine 415 | Ep. 167(Jer. 132) | 44 | pp.586-609 |
| Jerome 416 | Ep. 134(Aug. 172) | 56 | pp.261-263 |
| Jerome 418 | Ep. 141(Aug. 195) | 56 | pp.290-291 |
| Jerome 418 | Ep. 142(Aug. 123) | 56 | pp.291-292 |
| Jerome 419 | Ep. 143(Aug. 202) | 56 | pp.292-294 |

APPENDIX

| | | | |
|---|---|---|---|
| Augustine | Ep. 74(Jer. 111) | 34.2 | p.279 |
| Jerome | Ep. 126(Aug. 165) | 56 | pp.142-145 |

SUMMARY OF LETTERS
IN THEIR CHRONOLOGICAL CONTEXT


1) Ep. 28 starts as a letter of recommendation for Profuturus, the bearer of the letter. Unfortunately illness prevented him from setting off for Bethlehem and in fact, he never made the journey as he was then made bishop of Cirta, but Augustine did not realise immediately that this letter had not been delivered.[1] He later sent a copy of it to Jerome, together with Ep. 71. After praising Profuturus, Augustine continues on a more personal note, asking favours and giving advice concerning the translation of Greek Biblical exegetes such as Origen to make them available to Latin readers and concerning Jerome's translation of the Old Testament direct from the Hebrew instead of relying on the Septuagint. He then ventures to express his disagreement with Jerome's interpretation of Gal. 2.11-14,[2] confident of the truth of his own view and that Jerome will recognise his error. This criticism is accompanied by expressions of great admiration for Jerome and humility in desiring to be corrected by Jerome as a Biblical scholar whose authority he respects.


1. R. J. O'Connell (p. 11) is wrong to say that this letter turned up in Rome and elsewhere; he confuses Ep. 28 and Ep. 40.

2. See Jerome's commentary on Galatians 2.14 [P.L. 26.342].


2) Ep. 103 was given by Jerome to Praesidius to deliver to Augustine. It is a short letter of

recommendation and a token of friendship, in which
Jerome also alludes in vague terms to the difficulties
he is experiencing even in the monastic life which he
had chosen so as to avoid struggles with the devil; it
may be that he is covertly referring to the controversy
with John of Jerusalem.[1] He also mentions
Augustine's friend Alypius and refers to the fact that
both Augustine and Alypius have now been made bishops -
Alypius had moved from the monastic community at Hippo
to become bishop of his home town of Thagaste in 394
while Augustine had become bishop of Hippo in 396.

1. On Jerome and John of Jerusalem see e.g. Cavallera
and Kelly.

3) Ep. 40 was written in late 398 or early 399 when
Augustine realised (40.8) that Ep. 28 had never been
delivered. It therefore contains much repetition of the
contents of Ep. 28, including his exposition of the
Galatians passage, this time at even greater length.
He refers to a letter of some length from Jerome (now
lost) which was itself a reply to a letter from Alypius
to Jerome with a postscript from Augustine (also now
lost); no allusion is made to Ep. 103, so it is
possible that Augustine had not yet received this.
Augustine also brings up the problem of the title of
Jerome's work De Viris Illustribus, an untitled copy of
which he had recently received; he praises it but
expresses his puzzlement over the correct title, a
point which Jerome interpreted as an insult. He adds
some advice about the treatment of heretical authors in
this work and from his reaction (Ep. 112) it seems that
Jerome, with whom the attitude to heresy was a
sensitive subject, may have felt that Augustine was

questioning his orthodoxy, even though Augustine specifically says that he is certain Jerome holds the correct attitudes. Despite his queries and disagreements, Augustine is very laudatory of Jerome but he makes the mistake of jokingly asking Jerome to sing a palinode (in a reference to the early Greek poet Stesichorus): this is another point which filled Jerome with indignation and which he was to take up in Ep. 102 etc. This letter was entrusted to the deacon Paul who proved as unreliable a messenger as Profuturus.

4) Three years later Augustine had not yet had a reply to any of his questions; by now he knew that Jerome had received his Ep. 40 but he did not realise that it was only a copy, the original letter having been taken to Rome instead of Bethlehem and its contents spread around Italy before rumours about them reached Jerome. In this Ep. 67 Augustine himself refers to the rumour that he has written a book against Jerome and sent it to Rome - this he vehemently denies, unaware that the rumour in fact refers to Ep. 40. He expresses his wish that he and Jerome could live near each other and have frequent discussions, for he finds the problems of corresponding most frustrating and feels that letters are a poor substitute for personal contact.

5) Ep. 102 at last provides a relevant reply from Jerome, but even this does not engage with the literary and Biblical problems put forward by Augustine in Ep. 40. Instead Jerome concentrates on Augustine's attitude to him as he deduces it to be from the rumours and from the unsigned copy of Ep. 40 which have reached

him.  This letter has been provoked by the most recent
receipt of Augustine's Ep. 67 and Jerome asks the
messenger Asterius to wait so that he can write this
reply to it.  In it Jerome makes it clear that the book
referred to by Augustine (Ep. 67) was Ep. 40 and he
explains that Sisinnius had brought copies of it but
that he was unable to believe that it was really
written by Augustine and that was why he did not reply;
he regards his hesitation as proof of his love for
Augustine. (Another excuse for not replying sooner is
provided by Paula's illness which required Jerome to
devote himself to her care.)  In fact, Jerome is
apparently still unconvinced that Ep. 40 was written by
Augustine and he asks him to send an authenticated copy
or to admit openly that he did write it.  Jerome
rejects Augustine's invitation to criticise his works,
saying sarcastically that he has enough to do to defend
his own work; he is clearly very angry though his
indignation is slightly veiled by sarcasm and irony.
With an allusion to Persius he hints that Augustine
should be more concerned to correct his own faults than
to find fault with Jerome and he points out with
exaggerated irony that he is an old man and ought not
to be provoked by a mere youth.  Further Classical
references make it clear that he wishes to show that it
is not only Augustine who is learned enough to brandish
literary allusions; Jerome does not wish to be outdone
on any score.  Finally, as a parting shot, Jerome
refers to his reply to Rufinus' attack, enclosing the
third book of the Apology against Rufinus as a warning
to Augustine.

6)    Ep. 71 was written by Augustine and sent with
Cyprian before he received Jerome's furious Ep. 102,
for Augustine says he has not yet had a reply, despite
having sent Ep. 40 and Ep. 67.  To try to clear up the
situation he now also sends a copy of his first letter
(Ep. 28), showing how long he has been trying to elicit
an answer from Jerome, together with copies of Ep. 40
and Ep. 67 in case they never reached Jerome - for he
is still unaware of the fate of those letters.  Once
again he attempts to engage with Jerome on a point of
common concern and expresses his disappointment that
Jerome's translation of Job from the Hebrew is not as
carefully annotated with diacritical signs as was his
early translation from the Septuagint; in fact, he
wishes that Jerome would stick to translating from the
Greek, for fear that possible discrepancies between the
Greek and the Hebrew (and Jerome had indeed found many)
should cause the authority of Scripture to be doubted
and he cites the example of the incident at Oea (now
Tripoli).  Here, as throughout his writings, Augustine
maintains the supreme value of the Septuagint which was
used by the apostles and which he believed to be
inspired.


7) When Jerome wrote Ep. 105 it would seem that he had
received Augustine's Ep. 67 and a letter (now lost) in
which Augustine explained about Ep. 28, saying that he
gave it not only to Profuturus who was prevented from
delivering it by being made bishop (cf. Ep. 71), but
also to another man who was too afraid of the sea
voyage to undertake the journey to Bethlehem.  In this
letter Jerome is completely concerned with Augustine's
apparent attack on him and its effect on their

friendship. He expresses his irritation with Augustine's repeated demands for a reply to Ep. 40 and himself repeats what he said in Ep. 102 about Sisinnius bringing him a copy of it. He then criticises Augustine for lack of openness (in apparently attacking Jerome behind his back for Jerome still seems to believe that this was Augustine's intention with Ep. 40), and says that he did not reply to Ep. 40 because he was unwilling to criticise a bishop: all this is expressed even more ironically than in Ep. 102. In possible retaliation for what he regarded as aspersions cast on his orthodoxy, he then accuses Augustine of heretical ideas, in the politest terms, while repeating his reluctance to enter into a dispute because he is too old. He finishes the letter by expressing his unwillingness to be hypocritical - which is exactly what he is being in rejecting the idea, firmly held by Augustine, that friends should criticise each other: unlike Augustine, Jerome is not merely criticising his correspondent's views, but he is launching a bitter personal attack on him out of pique.

8) By the time Augustine wrote Ep. 73, in 404, he believed that Jerome had received his Ep. 71 which he had entrusted to Cyprian. Ep. 73 itself, delivered by Praesidius, was intended as a reply to Jerome's Ep. 102 and is therefore primarily concerned with the problems their friendship is encountering and with the rift between Jerome and Rufinus. Augustine strives to play down the venomous tone of Ep. 102, maintaining that (contrary to appearances!) it contained many indications of Jerome's benevolent and loving feelings towards him, although he admits that he found in it

also some signs that he had offended Jerome in some way (a definite example of understatement on Augustine's part). Here Augustine shows himself as stubborn as his opponent, insisting once again that he would welcome criticism, but he does feel that Ep. 102 was intended to cause unnecessary offence and that is not something which a true Christian friendship should permit. How can Jerome be sincere in his protestations about maintaining their friendship free from bitterness and suspicion if he can go out of his way to be offensive? Here Augustine has reached to the heart of the problem plaguing their incipient friendship and he is not afraid to speak freely about it (though Jerome will find such freedom of speech even less pleasant than the lack of openness of which he had unfairly accused Augustine). In fact he makes it clear that Jerome is responsible for jeopardising their friendship by taking offence at Ep. 40, where no offence was intended, and by trying to cause offence in Ep. 102.

Having stated his case firmly, Augustine does however attempt to defuse the situation by asking for forgiveness and thereby allowing Jerome a sense that he is in the right after all. Once again he expresses his frustration with the misfortunes dogging their correspondence, wishing that they did not live so far away from each other so that their letters could reach their destinations more quickly and surely. Also in a conciliatory vein, he expresses his admiration for Jerome's superior learning and even for his self-restraint in his reply to Rufinus' attack. But having read the work which formed the third book of Jerome's Apology against Rufinus, he admits that he is deeply shocked by the enmity which has developed between these two friends, formerly so intimate and feels it bodes

ill for all Christian friendships. He indirectly
requests Jerome not to publish attacks on Rufinus which
might prejudice the chances of their friendship
resuming - no doubt he also has in mind his own
friendship with Jerome and the threats to its
stability, for he continually moves between his concern
over their rift and his disappointment with Jerome's
thinly veiled threats in Ep. 102, with his
suspiciousness and readiness to retaliate rather than
accept any criticism. Augustine draws a tactful but
unfavourable comparison between his rather
uncomfortable relations with Jerome and the complete
confidence and trust he feels in the company of his
friends at Hippo and in passing, implies that Jerome
has somehow abandoned God, not being sufficiently
inflamed with Christian love.

It was after sending this letter that Augustine
received Jerome's Ep. 105, but he presumably did not
feel impelled to answer since it was to all intents and
purposes a repetition of Ep. 102. It is possible that,
though written earlier, it was only despatched with Ep.
112 in Cyprian's hands.


9) Ep. 112 at last provided a full-length reply to Ep.
40, now that Jerome had received Ep. 67 and Ep. 71, as
well as authorised copies of Ep. 28 and Ep. 40. Jerome
tries to guard against any criticism of it by stating
at the beginning that it is an impromptu reply,
composed in all haste while his messenger was eager to
leave - but Jerome had certainly had a long time to
ponder the questions Augustine had posed so long ago!
Although he now acknowledges that a reply is necessary,
he shows that he still regards Augustine's questions as

criticisms and he urges Augustine to concern himself with peace rather than victory in their discussions - advice which is perhaps more applicable to Jerome himself. This letter contains many references to and quotations from Augustine's earlier letters, now that Jerome is directly addressing the points raised by Augustine, concerning for example the title of his work De Viris Illustribus, his interpretation of Gal. 2.11-14 and his translation of the Old Testament from the Hebrew. With regard to the Galatians passage, Jerome defends his view that both Peter and Paul must have been pretending for he believes that Paul could not have reprimanded Peter for something of which he himself was guilty; he disclaims any originality (and therefore responsibility) for this view as he is merely following the interpretation of Origen and other Greek exegetes, while not necessarily endorsing their views. In a characteristically ironical manner Jerome denies that he has any authority of his own, but as he does not wish to appear to rely completely on his learned predecessors for his defence, he does attempt to argue his case using Scripture to support the view that even before this incident at Antioch, both Peter and Paul were aware that the law was not to be kept after the coming of Christ (in contradiction to Augustine's idea that the Jewish converts to Christianity were allowed to keep the law for a time even after Christ's grace had been revealed). Jerome then accuses Augustine of heresy again, holding tenaciously to his view that anyone who is subject to the law does not possess the Holy Spirit; far from accepting Augustine's criticism, he believes that Augustine will himself change his mind in the light of Jerome's evidence which is based on a different set of proof texts from Augustine's argument.

Finally he treats at some length the question (from Augustine's Ep. 71) of the difference in editing techniques used in his translations of the Old Testament from the Greek and the Hebrew and defends his methods of translation. He reiterates his plea for Augustine to leave him, an old man of no significance, in peace.

10) Jerome's Ep. 115, delivered by Firmus, appears to be a friendly postscript to Ep. 112, written shortly afterwards, probably on receipt of Augustine's Ep. 73. In this short letter Jerome sets aside all bitterness and recriminations, expressing his desire that they should send each other letters full of love instead of criticism and he conveys his warmest greetings to Augustine and his companions. He refers briefly to his commentary on Jonah which he had discussed at greater length in Ep. 112 and ends with the exhortation,'Let us sport on the field of Scripture without hurting one another'.

11) Augustine's Ep. 82 is a very long letter which forms the final stage in their discussion of the Galatians passage and it is written in reply to Jerome's Ep. 105, Ep. 112 and Ep. 115. Augustine refers to his letter Ep. 73 having been written a long time ago; he does not know whether it has reached Jerome but it appears that Augustine has recently received Ep. 115, delivered by Firmus, as well as Ep. 105 and Ep. 112 conveyed by Cyprian. He repeats some of what he had said in Ep. 73 about his reaction to the hostility between Jerome and Rufinus and then picks up

Jerome's final sentence from Ep. 115 which he apparently found somewhat offensive for he cannot see how, with Jerome's attitude to discussion, they can discuss things openly and fruitfully. He refers back to Jerome's Ep. 105, rejecting the expression, 'the honey-coated sword'. To show what his own attitude to discussion is, he continues with his policy of open criticism and takes Jerome to task for seeming to treat his own writings and those of earlier Biblical exegetes as if their authority was equal to that of Scripture, written by prophets and apostles, implying that Jerome is lacking in humility (and disregarding Jerome's statement in Ep. 112 that his own views have no authority).

This leads Augustine back to a lengthy discussion of Gal. 2.11-14 in the light of Jerome's defence of his views in Ep. 112. Again he vehemently denies that any of the apostles or prophets could be guilty of lying for any reason as this would undermine the authority of Scripture. This belief determines his attitude to all the arguments Jerome had put forth concerning Peter and Paul's behaviour. His own argument leads to a discussion of the value of Jewish law and a rejection of Jerome's accusation of heresy - in fact, he uses Jerome's technique of turning the tables on his opponent[1] by suggesting that Jerome's view of legitimate deceit on the part of the apostles is more heretical. Augustine clarifies his position by emphasising that the continued observance of the Jewish law was only legitimate for a short period after the coming of Christ (this was a point which Jerome had distorted to imply that Augustine was a supporter of the Jewish law), and he counters Jerome's barrage of Scriptural evidence in Ep. 112 with evidence of his own

that Christ himself respected certain Jewish rituals.
His view of the passage as a whole is that Peter and
Paul offer us a model in their open criticism,
compassion and humble acceptance of rebuke. In answer
to Jerome's list of Greek writers cited as
authoritative on this question, Augustine mentions
Ambrose and Cyprian in support of his views but claims
his only real authority is Paul himself. He ends this
discussion with a reference to Jerome's warning about
their friendship in Ep. 105 and with a renewed
expression of love, admiration and gratitude to Jerome.
Again he voices his belief that open, friendly
criticism is more beneficial than flattery and that
honesty need not lead to hatred; he apologises once
more for the misunderstanding over Ep. 40 and the
allusion to Stesichorus which so offended Jerome. His
letter ends with the admission that Jerome's arguments
have (at least) persuaded him of the value of
translation from the Hebrew - but he asks Jerome to
send a copy of his complete translation from the
Septuagint.

1. Cf. Jerome's use of this tactic in his Ep. 112 in
response to Augustine's suggestion that if the earlier
translators of Scripture could be mistaken, as Jerome
presumably believed, then so could Jerome himself, but
if they could not err, then Jerome's work was surely
superfluous.

12) After a break of about ten years their extant
correspondence resumes with Augustine's Ep. 166 in
which he consults Jerome on the problem of the origin
of the human soul and original sin which was so
important to their concerted attack on the central

issues of Pelagianism. In his introduction Augustine
alludes to Jerome's earlier reference to his old age:
the passing of time is revealed by Augustine's
statement that he, too, is now an old man but he still
feels very dependent on Jerome. He sets out the
various alternative views regarding the origin of the
soul and states what he is sure of as regards this
question (basing his beliefs firmly on certain
Scriptural passages such as Rom. 5.12) which he admits
to finding extremely problematic. He wishes to support
the creationist view also, he believes, held by Jerome
whereby it is thought that each soul is created
individually for each person at birth, but he finds
certain problems with this view e.g. where does the
soul contract the guilt by which it is condemned if a
person dies unbaptised? Other arguments against this
view he is able to refute, but the problem of infant
suffering he finds insurmountable and most agonising:
this is where he wants Jerome to help him. He quotes
from the third book of his work De Libero Arbitrio
(395) where he had offered some kind of answer to this
problem but which, he feels now, did not take
sufficient account of the problem of children who die
unbaptised. He cannot deny that souls are only saved
through Christ (certain Pelagians denied that baptism
was for the remission of sins) or that God is just, but
he again comes up against the unacceptable and
inexplicable (according to the creationist view)
suffering and damnation of infants. Augustine
concludes his letter with a profession of ignorance and
an appeal for enlightenment from Jerome.

13) Ep. 167 was delivered to Jerome by Orosius together with Ep. 166. Like Ep. 166 it in many ways resembles a treatise; this time the subject under discussion is the interpretation of James 2.10 which Augustine feels is of great relevance to our understanding of Christian morality. He asks Jerome to help him interpret it. Is it necessary, according to this text, to accept that all sins are equal, as the Stoics believed, even if the ancient philosophers' idea that all the virtues are inseparable is quite unconvincing? No, thinks Augustine, hereby confirming Jerome's rejection of the Stoic belief in his work against Jovinian, which Augustine had apparently read. Augustine also rejects the view that the person who possesses one virtue has them all, in favour of a view which allows for gradations of virtue. He explains the passage from the epistle of James by saying that anyone who acts contrary to love is guilty of all, for the commandment to love is paramount, although one person can still be considered more guilty than another if he commits a more serious sin. If Jerome does not agree with this interpretation, Augustine asks him to inform him - but Jerome did not apparently think it necessary to write back on this subject.


14) Jerome's Ep. 134 was written on receipt of Ep. 166 and Ep. 167 but not in direct reply to them,[1] though he does praise the contents of these two letters. It seems that he was not in complete agreement with them but he does not reopen the discussion; instead, he urges Augustine to join him in attacking Pelagius' dangerous doctrines. He hopes they can avoid arguing with each other (is this why he did not reply to

Augustine's queries?), for this might make their opponents think there exists ill-feeling between them: what is needed at the moment is a united front against Pelagianism. Jerome adds a postscript to his greeting, giving the lack of Latin copyists and 'someone's dishonesty' as the reasons for his inability to send his complete translation from the Septuagint, as Augustine had requested in Ep. 82.

1. In his Ep. 202A to Optatus, written in 419 or 420, Augustine mentions that he has never had a reply from Jerome to his questions about the origin of the soul.

15) Ep. 141 is a very brief letter in which Jerome praises Augustine warmly, if in rather enigmatic terms, for his success against the heretics who, he says, hate both of them intensely.

16) Ep. 142 is even more enigmatic and even shorter than Jerome's previous letter. Scholars have disagreed about the date of this letter, but it may refer to the Pelagians and date from roughly the same period as Ep. 141.

17) The final letter in the correspondence is Jerome's Ep. 143, apparently a reply to a letter (now lost) from Alypius and Augustine, in which they had asked whether Jerome had yet written attacking Annianus. Jerome refers to a letter written the previous year which the priest Innocent did not deliver; Jerome is glad that Alypius and Augustine wrote to him despite his apparent silence. He explains that he has not had a chance to

write a reply to Annianus because of his illness and
the death of Eustochium, but he hopes to be able to
write an attack on this heretic soon.  He finishes by
congratulating the two N. African bishops on their work
against the heresy of Caelestius, a supporter of
Pelagius.

# THEMES OF THE CORRESPONDENCE

## THE AUTHORITY OF THE SEPTUAGINT
Augustine's suspicion of Jerome's version of the Old
Testament from the Hebrew.

Augustine raised the question of the authority of the
Septuagint (a term applied not only to the Greek text
but also to the Latin translations made from it)
already in his first letter to Jerome, Ep. 28, and he
discussed it again in Ep. 71 and Ep. 82, while Jerome
defended his new version of the Old Testament from the
Hebrew in his Ep. 112. When Augustine composed Ep. 28
in 394 or 395, he had learned, possibly from Alypius,
that Jerome was now translating certain books of the
Old Testament direct from the Hebrew, rather than
revising them from the Septuagint as had been his
previous policy. In this letter Augustine expresses
briefly his worries over such an undertaking and asks
Jerome rather to continue his revision from Origen's
Hexapla version of the Septuagint, with its diacritical
signs marking divergences between the Septuagint and
the Hebrew. Augustine rather tentatively states his
belief in the supreme authority of the Septuagint[1]
and his distrust of the later translations from Hebrew
into Greek made by Aquila, Symmachus and Theodotion at
the instigation of the Jews who had come to mistrust

the Septuagint once the Christians started using it for
polemical purposes; Augustine feels that these
translations have too much of a Hebrew bias and that
they are surely superfluous, for it is unlikely (if one
accepts, as Augustine did, the story of its divinely-
inspired production) that the seventy or so original
translators of the Septuagint would have been mistaken,
experts as they were.

It seems that by this stage Jerome had completed
translations from the Hebrew of 1 and 2 Samuel, 3 and 4
Kings, Job, the Psalter and the Prophets; certainly,
his versions of Job and the Prophets were available in
Rome in 394 but it is unclear whether any of them had
actually reached Augustine. By 396 Jerome would have
also produced versions of Ezra, Nehemiah and 1 and 2
Chronicles. He had started on this work in around 390,
probably before he had completed his revision of all
the Old Testament books from the Hexapla Septuagint
which he had undertaken when he settled in Bethlehem.
His work on this project had led him to realise just
how problematic the Septuagint text was; not only was
there a wide divergency between different versions of
the Septuagint, but the Septuagint, on which all Latin
translations were based, differed in many points from
the Hebrew text which had become the official one.
Jerome came to believe that there could be no truth in
a text which had so many discrepancies[2] and he ceased
to believe that the Septuagint was inspired. In his
preface to the two books of Chronicles he states that a
new translation, direct from the Hebrew, would be
unnecessary if the Septuagint text were not so corrupt;
indeed, there seem to have been three different
versions being used in different parts of the Greek-
speaking Church, a fact which undermined the authority

universally (and most uncritically, in Jerome's view) accorded to it.

And yet Jerome repeatedly states that his new translation must not be regarded as intended to destroy the authority of the old, but as correcting its errors. Of course, many people[3] - not only Augustine - did see this as a direct challenge to the authority of the Septuagint and Jerome's new versions met with much opposition as they became available over a period of about fifteen years;[4] only Jerome's close followers supported him in his undertaking at first, although his version was gradually to take over from the Old Latin translation from the Septuagint.

Jerome was concerned to explain his intentions clearly to his detractors - as usual he did not like to be criticised! One of his chief arguments to his fellow Christians was that he had found that the Septuagint omits certain passages which are quoted from the Old Testament by Christ and the apostles. How can this be right? Jerome felt that it was shocking that such errors should be accepted through force of habit.[5] But it was not only in order to correct the text and clarify many passages that Jerome had undertaken his translation; he also saw it as having a polemical purpose. In his Apology against Rufinus he says that his version was intended to refute the Jews, for if Christians had a text based on the Hebrew, the Jews would be unable to use certain passages in their anti-Christian arguments which did not exist in the Septuagint; instead, the Christians could make sure that the Jews were hoist with their own petard, as it were.[6] It was necessary for Jerome to stress this anti-Jewish stance because he was apparently suspected of pro-Jewish tendencies in relying on the Hebrew text.

It is unlikely that Augustine read any of Jerome's arguments in favour of his translation during these years; certainly, he was not persuaded to relinquish his objections. Although Ep. 28 was not sent and only reached Jerome about ten years later in the form of a copy, Augustine brought up the subject again in Ep. 71, probably written in 403. He expresses his surprise to hear that Jerome has translated the book of Job from the Hebrew, although he has already produced a version of it from the Septuagint; he cannot understand why Jerome has omitted from the translation from the Hebrew the diacritical signs he had used so profitably in his earlier version. (Augustine here showed that he misunderstood the purpose of the obelisks and asterisks, a misunderstanding which will have irritated Jerome.) It appears that at this stage Augustine had at least seen a copy of the verion of Job from the Hebrew, although he does not seem actually to possess one.[7] He repeats his request for Jerome to abandon his translations from the Hebrew in favour of a revision of the Old Latin from the Septuagint, his main reason being that if the standard Latin text, based on the Septuagint, is replaced by a very different version, it will mean that the Greek and Latin-speaking churches will no longer be in harmony, for different texts of Scripture will be used in East and West and this could have dangerous consequences for a Church which was striving for unity on all fronts. Another problem with the new version was that if someone were to quibble about a certain word or passage, it would be difficult to defend the text because the Hebrew texts were not widely available and few Christians were Hebrew experts - they would therefore be forced to consult the Jews who, Augustine feels, are not to be trusted. Augustine had in fact heard of an incident which highlighted this problem, for he tells Jerome what had recently happened at Oea, where Jerome's version had apparently already been introduced in the church, but with negative results. Not only had the congregation, with whom the Old Latin version was culturally ingrained, rejected the new version because it was so different from the Septuagint, but when the Jews were consulted as to the propriety of the text, they supported the Septuagint and Latin version against Jerome's and the bishop at Oea was forced to correct a particular reading to calm the situation.[8] But if Augustine can think of a number of problems with Jerome's translation from the Hebrew, he seems to be perfectly content for Jerome to revise the Latin from the Septuagint and congratulates him on his success in this venture;[9] he admits that the divergent readings of the Septuagint do make it difficult to cite from it with authority.

At last, in 404, Jerome sent Augustine a reply to his objections. Although Ep. 112 is mainly concerned with Augustine's criticism of Jerome's commentary on Gal. 2.11-14, it does treat the question of the new translation of the Old Testament from the Hebrew in its last few pages. Jerome points out that diacritical signs are redundant in his new version and expresses a rather contemptuous surprise that Augustine is apparently using an edition of the Bible which contains Origen's obelisks and asterisks: surely, he adds sarcastically, if Augustine has so much respect for the 'original' Septuagint text, he should be ignoring those passages, indicated by an asterisk, which Origen added to the Septuagint from Theodotion's more literal translation from the Hebrew? But in fact, such uncorrupted versions are apparently rare. Jerome here also uses the same argument as he had used in his prefaces to the books of Job and Isaiah, namely that if one can accept a version incorporating the translations of Jews like Aquila, Symmachus and Theodotion, surely one should find the translation of a Christian (viz. Jerome) more acceptable, especially if it is free from Judaizing influences?

In answer to Augustine's doubts about Jerome being able to improve on the Septuagint, Jerome turns the argument against Augustine by applying the syllogism to Augustine's commentaries on the psalms: if the psalms are obscure, why should Augustine think he can improve on the explanations given by earlier exegetes, while if their meaning is obvious, why is there any need to augment the large number of existing commentaries by yet another one? Jerome implicitly denies the charge of arrogance implied by Augustine's objection and, as in the preface to Job, he plays down the pretensions of his work, saying that people can either take it or leave it, as long as they accept it for what it is.

In his reply to Ep. 112 Augustine returns to his doubts about Jerome's undertaking,[10] although he admits that he is now persuaded of the usefulness of such a translation, accepting at face value Jerome's modest proposal that it is only a supplement to the Septuagint. It is as if Jerome has enabled Augustine to see the complexity of the Scriptural tradition and has aroused his curiosity as to the elaborate ways in which the text has changed over the centuries, for Augustine continues by asking a number of questions, apparently now wanting advice and further information from one whom he recognises as an authority on the subject, rather than intending to object or criticise.

He does however cling to his devotion to the
Septuagint, requesting Jerome to send a copy of his
complete translation into Latin from the Septuagint so
that Augustine can revise his Latin translation,
avoiding the errors caused by the corrupt textual
tradition. He also continues to hold the belief that
the authority of the Septuagint must be upheld and that
in doubtful cases the text of the Septuagint should be
retained because of the weight of tradition behind it;
he still has more faith than Jerome in the skill of the
seventy translators and is only willing to accept
Jerome's new translation if it poses no fundamental
threat (though of course it did) to the authority of
the Septuagint and its translations.

It is clear that Augustine's main concerns were a
respect for tradition and dedication to the unity of
the Church against the onslaughts of various heresies.
He saw also the need to maintain the authority of
Scripture at a time when the Manichees, for example,
were undermining it by discrediting certain parts of
the Old Testament; he felt that Jerome's great project
would also discredit the Septuagint - and although his
respect for this text may seem naive, it was a respect
that had stood firm in the Church for centuries. It
would be unfair to depict Augustine, in this
controversy, as an unthinking stick-in-the-mud,
conservative by nature and without good reason; he had
good reasons for his views, as can be seen in these
letters to Jerome, and if he was less knowledgable and
less critical than Jerome, he was also more aware of
the Church's needs at the time and the repercussions of
Jerome's undertaking.(11)    Jerome's concerns were
perhaps less broad but he was obviously far superior to
Augustine in his linguistic and philological skills;

moreover, despite the opposition, he did manage to produce a sufficiently accurate, coherent and lucid translation - while sensibly rejecting the style of cultivated literary prose which he had originally admired so much - to enable him to be regarded as the most successful of the ancient translators.

1. On Augustine's attitude to the Septuagint, see Polman pp. 183-190; Cf. Aug. dCD 18.43 [CCL 48.638-40] on the authority of the Septuagint.

2. Cf. Jer. Pref. to Joshua, 'non possit verum esse quod dissonet.'

3. Jerome countered Rufinus' criticisms of his translation from the Hebrew in his Apology against Rufinus II.24-35 [CCL 79.60-72].

4. Jerome never translated those books which he had come to regard as deutero-canonical i.e.those O.T. books which were accepted in the Septuagint but not in the standard Hebrew text.

5. Jer. Pref. to Job.

6. Jer. Apol. cont. Ruf. II.25 [CCL 79.61-3]; cf. Pref. to Isaiah in Vulgate.

7. Cf. Aug. Ep. 71.3.

8. The reading in question was apparently that of 'ivy' instead of the accepted 'gourd' in Jonah 4, a reading which caused Jerome much trouble.

9. It is not clear which of these books Augustine had actually seen, or indeed how many of the Old Testament books Jerome had revised in this way.

10. See Aug. Ep. 82.34-5.

11. Cf. Aug. Quaest. in Gen. 169 [CCL 33.66]; dCD 18.43 [CCL 48.638-40] and 2.22 [CCL 47.55-6].

# THE INTERPRETATION OF GALATIANS 2.11-14

The central topic of Ep. 28, Ep. 40 and Ep. 82 from
Augustine, and Ep. 112 from Jerome is the question of
the interpretation of Gal. 2.11-14. The discussion was
apparently originally sparked off by Augustine's
reading of Jerome's commentary on Paul's letter to the
Galatians, written in 386 or 387 soon after Jerome
settled in Bethlehem. The passage at issue was one
which had been much discussed in the early Church for
the account given by Paul of his confrontation with
Peter at Antioch had opened the way for pagan and
heretical attacks on the apostles' behaviour which
seemed to discredit Christianity. The apologists'
problem lay in explaining how Peter, who had only a
short time before declared himself in favour of a
liberal attitude to the question of the Gentiles and
the Jewish law - whereby the Gentiles were not to be
forced to observe the law - could have acted so
inconsistently as to withdraw from the Gentiles after
he had eaten with them, just because a group of
Judaizing Christians turned up in Antioch. Was Peter
really afraid to offend these extremists by failing to
observe the law as they believed necessary? Did Paul
feel that Peter's behaviour betrayed the gospel and
threatened to divide the Church, for if Peter was seen
to support the Judaizing Christians, they might feel
they could demand that the Gentile Christians also be
subject to the law?

The early Christians responded to these problems in
different ways. It seems that Tertullian, Cyprian,[1]
Ambrose and Hilary all took Paul's account at face

value and defended Paul for rebuking Peter, with
Cyprian taking the passage as showing how admirable
Peter was in his humble acceptance of rebuke. Clement
of Alexandria,[2] however, put forward an ingenious
explanation of this embarrassing incident, namely that
the Cephas mentioned in this passage did not refer to
the apostle Peter but to one of the seventy disciples
with the same name; few were to find this explanation
convincing. But an alternative explanation, proposed
by Origen, did convince Jerome, at least until
Augustine made clear the dangers and problems inherent
in this view. Origen initiated the theory that Peter
and Paul had agreed to stage the dispute to keep both
the Gentile and the Jewish Christians happy, because
Paul's criticism of Peter's Judaizing behaviour would
seem to support the Gentiles, while Peter's withdrawal
from the Gentiles would appear to support the Jewish
Christians. But as Augustine and others saw, this
theory laid the apostles open to a charge of dishonesty
which Augustine regarded as far more serious than the
charge of inconsistency originally levelled at them.

When Augustine read Jerome's interpretation he was
outraged and became determined to win Jerome's support
for his own view - indeed, he maintained his polemical
stance on this issue for ten years until his Ep. 82
closed the dispute with Jerome. Cole-Turner has shown
that Augustine had already focussed on this passage of
Galatians in his debates with the Manichees and
Donatists at this period; in fact Ep. 28 was written at
about the same time as Augustine's own interpretation
of the letter to the Galatians and his work On
Falsehood (DE MENDACIO), in which he discusses the
problems highlighted in his dispute with Jerome, and at
a time of confrontation with the Manichees, while Ep.

82, his final word on the matter in his discussion with Jerome, was written during a period of anti-Donatist debate. During his debates with the Manichees Augustine was concerned with the authority of Scripture because the Manichees believed that any apparent problems in the texts are only problems of faulty interpretation. Augustine was therefore worried that Jerome's exegesis of Gal. 2.11-14 would undermine the authority of Scripture because it allowed apparently unacceptable behaviour in the Bible to be explained away as insincere or performed for a laudable motive - a case of the end justifying the means. Augustine himself believed that it was more important for Scripture always to be reliable than for its protagonists always to be seen to behave impeccably; while fear of the Judaizing Christians was acceptable on the part of Peter, it would be absolutely unacceptable, in Augustine's view, if Paul were to be seen to be dishonest in his account or if both apostles were to be seen to act deceitfully.

So while Jerome takes the view that Peter and Paul cannot really have been in dispute, otherwise Paul would have been acting inconsistently in rebuking Peter for something of which he, Paul, was himself guilty (i.e. observing certain points of the Jewish law), Augustine read the passage in a literal sense, convinced that Paul really did condemn Peter and that Peter really was in the wrong for seeming to compel the Gentiles to obey the law. He does not deny that Paul observed certain Jewish rituals[3] but he tries to explain this to Jerome by saying that Paul did so because it was permissible at that time i.e. shortly after the coming of Christ, for Christians coming from the Jewish faith; this did not imply, however, that observance of the Jewish law was necessary, either for Jews or Gentiles, after the coming of Christ. For Augustine the central issue in this dispute is the question of the authority of Scripture and the danger that Jerome's interpretation will justify the use of lies and deceit; for Jerome the main problem is the question of how long the Jewish law pertained in the nascent Church and whether the apostles, as Jews converted to Christ, ever kept the Jewish law after their conversion. He believed that after the coming of Christ the Jewish law was not only dead but even deadly to all who practised it (Jerome often quotes in support of this view), while Augustine held to the view that there were two phases, not just one, in the abolition of the law: for a short while after the coming of Christ observance of the law by Jewish Christians was acceptable, as long as they did not believe that observance was necessary for salvation; after this short period, the law would be as deadly to Jewish Christians as to Gentiles.

Needless to say, Jerome used this to accuse Augustine of being pro-Jewish and indeed heretical, but it was Augustine's view which won the day and which seems to have been almost universally accepted by the Church. Aquinas[4] for example, in giving an outline of the debate between Jerome and Augustine, comes down in favour of Augustine and agrees with him (probably following Cyprian) that this passage of Galatians is intended to offer us Peter and Paul as examples of humility and respectful frankness. But whatever view one takes, this dispute focusses on a Scriptural passage of abiding interest, touching on a number of important issues. It is fascinating to witness Jerome and Augustine's reactions to it - reactions which were in many ways typical of each of them and of their concerns and personal circumstances, but which also shed light on broader historical issues, such as the exegetical tradition in the early Church and the ever-present threat of heresy.

1. Tertullian Adv. Marc. I.20, IV.3 [CSEL 47.315, 427]; Cyprian Ep. 71 [CSEL 3.2.773]. For contemporary views of the problem cf. Ambrosiaster in his commentary on Galatians [P.L. 17.349f.].

2. Clement Hypotyp. apud Euseb. H.E. I.12.2 [ed. Schwartz I.82].

3. Cf. Aug. Cont. Faust. Manich. 19 [CSEL 25.1.496-535], in which he uses this as a means of defending the Old Testament against Manichaean attack.

4. Aquinas S. Th. I. II. q. 103 a4 ad 1; in Ep. ad Galatas.

# THE ORIGIN OF THE HUMAN SOUL

The problem of the origin of man's soul was one which had exercised pagan philosophers as well as Christian theologians and which allowed of no easy resolution, especially for Christians, as the Bible offered little information on this question which could form the basis of any orthodox theory. It is therefore hardly surprising that even Augustine found this issue problematic and that he wrestled with it on and off throughout his life, without apparently ever reaching a definite conclusion which could satisfy all the problems raised by the possible solutions. In his Retractationes (II.45) Augustine speaks of this question as 'very hard to fathom' (res obscurissima) and elsewhere in the same work (I.1.3) he says that as to the question of how the soul is produced for each individual, he neither knew the answer when he wrote his work against the Academics back in 386 nor does he know it now (shortly before his death in 430).[1]

Jerome, too, clearly had problems, though he is less frank about his difficulties and ignorance on the question when it comes up in discussion, whether with Rufinus, with Marcellinus and Anapsychia or with Augustine himself; he manages to avoid the subject as far as possible and it is hard to see which position he felt closest to. Augustine, on the other hand, does discuss the question on a number of occasions, of which the discussion in his Ep. 166 to Jerome is probably the most thorough;[2] it shows him at an interesting stage in the development of his thought on original sin (on which he focusses in considering the different theories about the soul's origin) and presents him as more compassionate and hesitant than he is sometimes given credit for by those who regard him as harsh and dogmatic.

By the end of the fourth century it seems that there were five main theories as to the soul's origin, to which Jerome refers in his letter (Ep. 126) to Marcellinus and Anapsychia who consulted him on the subject in about 411. One theory was that souls fell from the sky and were imprisoned in the body as a punishment for sins committed before their incarnation: this was apparently the view held by Pythagoreans and Platonists and they were followed by Origen who adapted the theory for Christian doctrine. Another theory, held by Stoics, Manichees and the Priscillianists, was that the soul was a part of God and therefore immortal. Jerome refers to a theory, held by 'certain men of the Church' (but which he himself pours scorn on), to the effect that souls, created by God, pre-exist their sojourn in the body and are kept in a sort of storehouse until their incarnation in each individual body. Another view which he dismisses but which has a strong tradition within the Church and was held, according to Jerome, by Tertullian,[3] Apollinaris and many others, is the so-called traducianist theory, whereby it is believed that the soul, whether regarded as spiritual or material, is handed down by the parents to the children.[4] If, in this letter, Jerome admits to supporting any view, it is the one which states that each soul is created by God from nothing for each individual at conception or birth; certainly this is the view which Augustine takes him to favour and which Augustine himself tries to accept in Ep. 166, though he admits it involves certain problems for Christian

theology. Rufinus, too, had thought that this was
Jerome's view of the soul, as is clear from Jerome's
Apology against Rufinus,[5] written in 402. It seems
likely that Jerome was able to hold the creationist
belief, at least at first, because the doctrine of
original sin had not been central to his point of view;
and when Augustine later presented to him the
complexities of this view, he refrained from discussing
such a difficult subject - in future, when the subject
came up, he would refer people to Augustine's Ep. 166.

It is clear that this was a perennial subject for
discussion and one which was much in evidence at the
time of Jerome and Augustine's correspondence with each
other. Augustine had in fact discussed this problem in
his writings even before he began to correspond with
Jerome and many years before he composed Ep. 166.
Already in the De Genesi contra Manichaeos of 388/9
Augustine had used the crucial, if sparse, texts of
Gen. 1.26-7 and Gen. 2.7 to show that the human soul is
not part of the divine nature, and in the third book of
his work on free will he puts forward four possible
theories of the soul's origin - omitting the one
recorded by Jerome whereby souls pre-exist in a sort of
store - but without pronouncing himself in favour of
any theory in particular. In this widely-read work he
also brings up the problem of infant death and
suffering which he was to discuss in Ep. 166 in
connection with the question of the soul's origin and
the problem of the transmission of original sin.

In Ep. 166, however, written more than twenty
years later at a time when Pelagius was winning people
over to his views on grace and original sin, Augustine
shows that he is more desperate to find an answer to
these problems, now that he is having to define his

views more clearly in reaction to Pelagius. His appeal
to Jerome for information and support does nevertheless
reveal his doubts and hesitations and if he declares
that he is very keen to agree with Jerome and accept
the creationist view of the soul, he does admit that
this view presents what appears to him an
insurmountable problem, namely that it fails to explain
the transmission of original sin. If sin is not
present in the new-born child, how can it be right for
the soul of such a child who dies in infancy to be
damned? Above all, Augustine clings to the belief,
based on Rom. 5.12 and 1 Cor. 15.22, that in Christ
alone is our hope of salvation and that the grace of
Christ necessary for salvation is bestowed only by
baptism in the Catholic Church. Again and again in the
course of the letter Augustine comes up against the
problem of defending divine love if unbaptised infants
are damned without committing sin or defending divine
justice if sin is not somehow transmitted even to the
new-born child. But how can the creationist theory
help? Surely only the traducianist theory or Origen's
belief in pre-natal sin can explain how it is just for
infants to be damned? These problems clearly caused
Augustine a great deal of anguish; he can deal with
some of the objections to the creationist theory, but
not this fundamental one of reconciling God's justice,
the universal need for grace through baptism and the
creationist theory.(6)

It is possible that Augustine was tempted, in his
desire to combat the Pelagian denial of the
transmission of original sin, to espouse the
traducianist theory, but he does not do so in this
letter; he did discuss it at some length a couple of
years later in Ep. 190 to Optatus, but even here he

seems as much of an agnostic as he does in his other works.[7]   Certainly Ep. 166 did not contain anything with which Jerome could find fault; the only response Augustine received from his correspondent was a brief expression of admiration (in Jerome's Ep. 134) for the long letter which Paulus Orosius had delivered to Bethlehem.   Augustine waited in vain for a full-scale defence of the creationist theory but at least his professions of ignorance were treated with respect by Jerome, a respect which contrasts sharply with the fiercely scornful reaction Jerome had accorded to Rufinus' vagueness on the subject.[8]

The failure of Jerome and Augustine to engage in a proper discussion on this subject seems in fact to have led someone, possibly in the early Middle Ages, to construct a spurious and fictitious dialogue between the two great authorities:[9]   this short piece relies heavily on verbatim extracts from their works, especially from Ep. 166. and although it may be said to provide a useful summary of their views, it does not bring the reader any closer to a solution of the problem.   Neither is it a well-structured composition, for Jerome's brief pronouncements are often completely irrelevant to the point Augustine has just made;   in fact this attempt to construct a dialogue merely emphasises Jerome's failure to express himself on the subject and Augustine's inability to bring the discussion to a satisfactory conclusion.

1. Cf. Aug. Ep. 180 in which he cuts short a discussion on the subject in his letter to Oceanus by saying, 'There is no need for me to say any more since you know what I mean, or rather what I do not mean'.

2. O'Daly, however, considers that it 'adds little to the extensive if inconclusive speculation of the De Genesi ad Litteram'.

3. Cf. Tertullian De Anima 23-27, 36 [CCL 2.815-24, 838-9].

4. A view which was apparently rejected by Jerome in his commentary on Eccles. 12.7 [CCL 72.357].

5. Jer. Apol. cont. Ruf. III.28-31 [CCL 79.99-102].

6. Cf. Aug. Ep. 180.2.

7. Cf. Aug. Ep. 190.16-17.

8. Cf. Rufinus Apol. ad Anastasium 6 [CCL 20.27]; Jer. Apol. contra Ruf. II.8-10 [CCL 79.40-3].

9. Ep. 37 seu dialogus sub nomine Hieronymi et Augustini [P.L. 30.262-271].

# THE INTERPRETATION OF JAMES 2.10

Together with his Ep. 166 Augustine entrusted Orosius
with another long letter for Jerome; this was his Ep.
167 in which he aired his views on the possible
interpretation of the verse in which St.James writes
that anyone who keeps the whole law but fails in one
point is guilty of all. Again he appeals to Jerome for
guidance but as with Ep. 166, Jerome remained silent
and we cannot come to any conclusion as to what his
thoughts on the problematic passage were. It seems
possible that Augustine's letter was inspired by his
worries over the Pelagian attitudes to sin and grace
which were spreading through the Church at this time;
certainly, part of the reason for sending Orosius with
the letters was so that the young man could learn from
Jerome and also apprise him and the church at Jerusalem
of the anti-Pelagian struggle in Africa;[1] this was a
period of intensive anti-Pelagian activity, in which
both Jerome and Augustine were involved and the
question of the orthodoxy or heresy of Pelagius' ideas
still hung in the balance. Augustine does not refer
specifically to Pelagius in Ep. 166 although he
mentions the problem of infant guilt (Ep. 167.2) and
his discussion of the Stoic theory that all sins are
equal[2] may be connected with Pelagian ideas: in his
Ep. 43 Jerome ascribes Pelagian errors on sin to the
influence of Stoic and Pythagorean ideas of man's
ability to subdue the passions and live without sin by
means of his own will.[3] It seems that Pelagius was
emphasising that all God's commandments must be
observed without exception i.e. that man, in his

struggle for virtue, should avoid committing even minor sins, as well as more serious ones. In this way he could be seen to be supporting the Stoic theory, and indeed the verse in question in Augustine's letter does seem to lend support to the Stoic and Pelagian views. This is the problem which Augustine was keen to resolve in Ep. 167 and with Jerome's advice, for he regards a clear explanation of James 2.10 as crucial to the question of Christian morality (Ep. 167.2).

After appealing to Jerome for some explanation of this verse, Augustine continues by setting out his own thoughts and difficulties. He starts by considering the verse in its context and then points to the apparent parallel between St. James' saying and the theories of the ancient philosophers about the inseparableness of the virtues and the equality of all sins. He agrees with what Jerome had written in his work against Jovinian, namely that Christians cannot believe in the equality of sins, but this brings him up against the problem (Ep. 167.5) of reconciling the fact that whereas the virtues do indeed seem to be inseparable, sins are not all equal. By appealing to a combination of philosophical ideas, Scriptural authority and commonsense, Augustine takes a critical look at these theories and manages to show that the Stoic theory has to be rejected, despite its plausibility; he argues that sins are more numerous than virtues and some sins or faults are contrary to one another because some are the complete opposite of a virtue while others closely resemble it - for example, wastefulness is a fault which is the opposite of the virtue thrift, while stinginess resembles thrift but is a fault, not a virtue, but it would be contradictory to say that some one who is wasteful is necessarily also stingy, as the Stoic theory would imply. Furthermore, one vice can be replaced by another, but the theory that one vice implies all others would not allow this.

Having rejected this theory, Augustine goes on to express his doubts about the more attractive theory that one virtue embraces and implies all others;[4] as no one can be without sin in this world, a Christian cannot believe that if he has one virtue he has them all for this would imply that he was without sin. Instead, he ventures to give an alternative explanation which will be both realistic and true to Scripture: virtue is not an indivisible point but something in which progress can be made (Ep. 167.12-13) and which one person can have more of, another less. But what then is the one point referred to by St. James, which makes us guilty of everything if we fail in it? Augustine suggests that this is love, for is not love the answer to all the commandments, is it not the supreme virtue? If a man does not love God and his fellow man, he cannot hope to fulfil any of the commandments or be called virtuous and by offending against any of the commandments, he is guilty of contravening love. However, it is possible to be either more or less guilty, even if it is true, as St. James says, that one is guilty of everything. Augustine ends his discussion on a more practical note, bearing in mind that he was concerned to show how James 2.10 was relevant to Christian morality: basing himself on St. James' words, he proposes that the Christian must strive to love all men without prejudice, but because every man does fail to some extent in fulfilling the commandment to love, we must try, by showing mercy and forgiveness, to redress the balance and to deserve God's mercy and forgiveness.

The final paragraph of the letter makes it clear that his proposal is only tentative and that he would welcome support or correction from Jerome.

It seems that the subject of this letter remained prominent in Augustine's mind, for some time later, possibly after Jerome had given his brief approval of this letter in Ep. 134, Augustine composed a sermon, recently discovered,[5] in which he gives an explanation, aimed at his congregation, of this verse, James 2.10. The treatment and style are different, the conclusion similar. Here, too, Augustine rejects the idea that the petty thief is equal to the adulterer or murderer and suggests that because the whole law is summed up in the precepts to love God and our neighbour, he who sins against love is guilty of everything; in fact, even the thief and the adulterer sin against love and so they are both guilty of everything because they both violate the root of everything, but the thief is less guilty, the adulterer more. Even the conclusion to the sermon closely resembles Ep. 167 in that Augustine consoles his congregation by saying that although we are too weak, even after baptism, to avoid all faults, we can nevertheless be saved from the consequences of our sins if we show mercy to others and pray sincerely that God forgive us as we forgive others. In both works Augustine puts something of an anti-Pelagian slant on the text, for instead of using it to urge the danger of sin and the importance of a life of virtue, he characteristically places the whole emphasis on love of God and neighbour, thereby giving an original interpretation.[6]

1. This led to a conference at Jerusalem at which both Orosius and Pelagius were present but where Pelagius was able to argue his way out of Orosius' accusation.

2. Modern commentators tend to regard Augustine's linking of this verse to Stoic and other ancient philosophical theories as irrelevant; instead, they assert, the verse is connected with rabbinical writings among which there are many examples of sayings expressed in a similar formula and with a similar used of emphasis. Dibelius, however, in his commentary on the epistle of St. James, (Der Brief des Jakobus, (Göttingen, 11th ed. 1964)) takes a more sympathetic view of Augustine's treatment, for he recognises that there may indeed be a connection between Jewish ideas and Stoic theories and that Philo, for example, may be regarded as attempting to harmonise them. Cf. Hicks who draws a parallel between the Stoic view of sins and the Christian attitude expressed by St. Paul in the words, 'Whatever is not of faith is of sin' and by what James writes in his epistle, 2.10.

3. Cf. Ep. 148 attributed to Jerome [CSEL 56.334] but possibly written by Pelagius, in which the Stoic theory that all sins are equal is discussed in connection with the Christian attitude to sin.

4. On this as a Stoic theory, see Sandbach pp. 41-45.

5. Ed. A. Wilmart, in Rev. d'Ascét. et de Mystique II (1921) 351-372.

6. Cf. the interpretation of Aquinas who explains this verse by saying that in sinning man shows contempt of God who is the source of the whole law; any sin which a man commits makes him guilty of such contempt.

# TEXT AND TRANSLATION OF THE CORRESPONDENCE

The text used for this translation is basically that contained in the C.S.E.L. editions. The letters of Jerome were edited in three volumes by Isidor Hilberg (Vienna 1910-1918) and those of Augustine in four volumes (34/1, 34/2, 44, 57) by Goldbacher (Vienna 1895-1911), with a fifth volume (58) containing the editor's preface and indices. Any significant divergences from the text are signalled in the notes.

In an appendix are included two letters which touch on the correspondence: Ep. 74 from Augustine to Praesidius, written in 404, in which Augustine asks Praesidius to make sure that Jerome receives Ep. 73; he also encloses copies of Ep. 67 and Jerome's Ep. 102 to show Praesidius how restrained he has been in the face of Jerome's invective: this letter thus reveals something of Augustine's attitude to his correspondence with Jerome. The other letter is Jerome's Ep. 126 to Marcellinus and Anapsychia, written in 411 in reply to their request for enlightenment concerning the knotty problem of the origin of the human soul: Jerome refers them to Augustine as being more capable of explaining this matter, so this letter may have been partly responsible for Augustine's attempts, a few years later, to grapple with the problem in his Ep. 166.

On the history of the text and the manuscripts, see H. Lietzmann, Zur Entstehungsgeschichte der Briefsammlung Augustins (Sitz. Ber. der Preuss. Akad. der Wiss. phil. hist. Kl. (Berlin 1930) pp. 356-388). On the question of the dating of the letters of this correspondence, see Cavallera vol. II pp. 47-50 and De

Bruyne, as well as the introduction to Schmid's Latin
edition of their correspondence. A summary of the
textual tradition of Augustine's letters is given in
the introduction by M. Pellegrino to the edition of the
letters, with Italian translation, (Citta Nuova vol. I
(Rome 1969) pp. xxi-xxv).

There have been a number of earlier translations of
the letters of Jerome and Augustine (either complete or
selections from the corpus) into English, but there
exists no translation of the complete correspondence
between Jerome and Augustine. Modern translations into
English of Jerome's letters include that by C. C.
Mierow in vols. 31-33 (1960-1963) of the series of
Ancient Christian Writers, and the selection by F. A.
Wright (which does not include any of the letters to
Augustine) produced for the Loeb Classical Library
(1933 repr. 1980). A complete, if faulty, translation
of Augustine's letters exists in the Fathers of the
Church series, volumes 12,18,20,30 and 32, made by
Sister W. Parsons, while selections are available in
the translation by J. G. Cunningham (Library of the
Fathers, 1872-5) or by J. H. Baxter for the Loeb
Classical Library (1930 repr. 1965). My translation
tries to remain faithful to the rather formal style of
Jerome's and Augustine's letters to each other, while
avoiding such circumlocutions as their references to
each other as 'your prudence' etc. which sound strange
in English. My other aim has been clarity in the often
complex arguments and allusive style they use in
expressing their ideas and beliefs; this aim has
involved occasional paraphrases to clarify the writers'
more elliptical expressions.

In giving the numbers of the psalms to which Jerome
and Augustine refer in their letters I shall give both

the numbering used in the Vulgate (which followed the Septuagint edition) and that of the modern Revised Standard Version (which follows the Hebrew numbering). In referring to authors, details of whose works are listed in the Bibliography, I shall mention only their name and the relevant page reference.

## BIBLIOGRAPHY

Antin, P. (ed.): Jérôme, Commentaire sur Jonas (Sources Chrétiennes 43, Paris 1956)

Aquinas, Thomas: Commentary on Galatians, Super epistolas S. Pauli lectura vol. 1 (Rome 1953) 582-4

Auvray, P: Saint Jerome et Saint Augustin. La controverse au sujet de l'incident d'Antioche, RechSR 29 (1939) 594-610

Barberiis, Philippe de: Discordantiae SS. Hieronymi et Augustini (Rome 1481)

Bindesboll, S: Augustinus et Hieronymus de S. Scriptura ex Hebraeo interpretanda disputantes (Copenhagen 1825)

Bonner, G: Rufinus of Syria and African Pelagianism, AugStud 1 (1970) 31-47

Idem: St. Augustine of Hippo, Life and Controversies (2nd ed. Norwich 1986)

Bright, W: Select anti-Pelagian treatises of St. Augustine (Oxford 1880)

Brown, P: Augustine of Hippo, a biography (London 1967)

62

Cavallera, F: Saint Jérôme, sa vie et son oeuvre, 2 vols, (Louvain 1922)

Chadwick, H: The Early Church (London 1967)

Cole-Turner, R: Anti-heretical Issues and the Debate over Galatians 2. 11-14 in the letters of St. Augustine to St. Jerome, AugStud 11 (1980) 155-166

De Bruyne, D: Les anciennes collections des épîtres de S. Augustin, Rev. Ben. 43 (1931) 284-295

Idem: La correspondance echangée entre Augustin et Jérôme, ZntW 31 (1932) 233-248

De Vathaire, J: Les relations de saint Augustin et de saint Jérôme, Misc. Agost. 1930 pp. 484-499.

Dorsch, E: St. Augustinus und Hieronymus ueber die Wahrheit der Biblischen Geschichte, ZKTh 35 (1911) 421-448 and 601-664

Dufey, A: Controverse entre s. Jérôme et s. Augustin d'après leurs lèttres, Revue du clergé francais 25 (1901) 141-149

Fleury, Abbé: Ecclesiastical History (transl. J. H. Newman, Oxford 1843)

Ferguson, J: Pelagius, a historical and theological study (Cambridge 1956)

Gruetzmacher, G: Hieronymus, 3 vols. (Leipzig 1901-8)

Haren, M: Medieval Thought (London 1985)

Hicks, R. D: Stoic and Epicurean (London 1910)

Hritzu, J. N: The style of the letters of Saint Jerome (Washington 1939)

Hunt, E. D: Holy Land pilgrimage in the later Roman Empire AD 312-460 (Oxford 1982)

Kelly, J. N. D: Jerome (London 1975)

La Bonnardiere, A-M: Augustin a-t-il utilise la 'Vulgate' de Jérôme?, in Saint Augustin et la Bible, ed. A-M. La Bonnardière (Paris 1986)

Lagrange, R. P: Mélanges d'histoire religieuse (Paris 1915) 167-186

Lardet, P. (ed.): Jérôme, Contra Rufinum (Sources Chrétiennes 303, Paris 1983)

Lietzmann, H: Zur Entstehungsgeschichte der Briefsammlung Augustins, Sitz. Ber. der Preuss. Akad. der Wiss. phil. hist. Kl.(Berlin 1930) 356-388, esp. 374-382

Lightfoot, J: Commentary on Galatians (10th ed. London 1890)

Malfatti, E: Una controversia tra S. Agostino e S. Girolamo, La Scuola Cattolica 1921 pp. 321-338, 402-426

Moehler, J. A: Hieronymus und Augustinus im Streit über Gal. 2.14, in Gesammelte Schriften und Aufsätze, Bd. 1, (Regensburg 1839) 1-18

Mueller, W. G: Der Brief als Spiegel der Seele, Antike und Abendland 26 (1980) 138-157

O'Connell, R. J: Augustine's rejection of the fall of the soul, AugStud 4 (1973) 1-32

O'Daly, G. J. P: Augustine on the origin of souls, Festschrift H. Doerrie, Jahrbuch fuer Antike u. Christentum, Ergaenzungsbd. 10 (Muenster 1983) 184-191

Overbeck, F: Ueber die Auffassung des Streites des Paulus mit Petrus in Antiochen bei den Kirchenvätern (Basel 1877)

Idem: Aus dem Briefwechsel des Augustinus mit Hieronymus, Historische Zeitschrift 6 (1879) 222-259

Parsons, Sr. W: A Study of the Vocabulary and Rhetoric of the Letters of St. Augustine (Washington 1923)

Pasquali, G: Storia della tradizione e della critica del testo (Florence 1934) 451-6

Peter, H: Der Brief in der roemischen Literatur, Abhandl. der Sächs. Akad. der Wiss. IX.20 (1907)

Polman, A. D. R: The Word of God according to Augustine (London 1961)

Sandbach, F. H:   The  Stoics  (Ancient  Culture  and
Society, London 1975)

Schmid, J. (ed.):   SS. Eusebii Hieronymi et Aurelii
Augustini epistulae mutuae, in Florilegium Patristicum
22 (Bonn 1930)

Semple, W. A:   Some letters of St. Augustine, BJRL 33
(1950) 111-130

Simard, G:   La querelle de deux saints: saint Jérôme et
saint Augustin, Rev. de l'univ. d'Ottawa 12 (1942) 15-
38

Thraede,     K:         Grundzuege     griechisch-roemischer
Brieftopik (Munich 1970)

Tourscher, F. E:   The correspondence of St. Augustine
and  St.  Jerome,  American  Ecclesiastical  Review  57
(1917) 476-492, 58 (1918) 45-56

Vaccari, A:   Cuore e stile di S. Agostino nella lettera
73, Misc. Agost. II 353-358

Wankenne, L. J:   La langue de la correspondance de S.
Augustin, Rev. Bén. 94 (1984) 102-153

Wilmart, A:   Un sermon de saint Augustin, Rev. d'ascét.
et Myst. 2 (1921) 351-372

AUGUSTINE EP. 28

Never has anyone known another man's features as
well as the peaceful joy of your studies in the Lord
and your truly noble application to them are known to
me. And so, although I have a great desire to be fully
acquainted with you, it is nonetheless only a small
part of you with which I am not so familiar, namely
your physical presence; and after my most blessed
brother Alypius[1] (now a bishop but already at that
time worthy of the episcopate) saw you and was then
seen by me on his return, I cannot deny that his
account has enabled me to form a pretty clear
impression even of your physical appearance; and even
before his return, when he was seeing you there, I saw
you, but through his eyes. For anyone who knew us
would say that he and I were not two in mind but only
in body[2] at least as far as harmony of ideas and
loyal friendship are concerned, though not with regard
to merit in which he surpasses me. And so, because you
loved me first of all in the spirit which we share and
through which we strive for the same thing, and you
now love me as a result of his recommendation, it is by
no means impolite of me, as it would be if I were a
complete stranger, to commend to you, my dear brother,
our brother Profuturus; I hope that through my efforts
and then with your assistance he will truly profit
you,[3] unless perhaps my efforts will do no good
because he is the sort of person who is likely to give
you a better recommendation of me than I of him. I
ought perhaps to stop writing at this point if I could
be satisfied with the usual formal letter; but my mind
is bubbling over with thoughts I want to share with you

about the studies we are pursuing in our Lord Jesus
Christ, who deigns, also by means of your love, to
supply us generously with many benefits and provisions,
so to speak, for the journey which he has revealed to
us.

I therefore venture to ask - and all the learned
members of the African churches join me in asking -
that in translating the works of those Greek scholars
who have discussed our Scriptures in such an excellent
way, you should not be reluctant to devote care and
attention to the task. For you are in a position to
allow us also to become familiar with such writers -
and one especially[4] whom you mention with particular
pleasure in your writings. But when it comes to
translating the sacred canonical writings into Latin, I
would like you simply to do what you did when you
translated the book of Job,[5] in other words to add
signs indicating the points where your translation
differs from that of the Septuagint, which has such
great authority. I would be very surprised if anything
could still be found in the Hebrew texts which had
escaped the notice of all those translators who were
such experts in that language. I say nothing of the
Seventy[6] for I would not dare to give any kind of
decisive answer to the question of whether they
possessed a greater harmony of wisdom or of inspiration
than one man could have, but I do think that their work
should without doubt be accorded preeminent authority
in this field. I am more disturbed by those[7] who, in
making later versions, clung more tenaciously, as the
saying goes,[8] to the method and rules of Hebrew words
and expressions and not only disagreed amongst
themselves but also left out many things which had to
be explained and elucidated much later. If these

things are obscure, one must suppose that you, too, can be mistaken about them; if they are obvious, it is most unlikely that those translators could have been mistaken about them. I would therefore beg you to give me assurances with regard to this matter by kindly explaining your position on it.

I have also read certain writings which are said to be by you, on the epistles of the apostle Paul: in your commentary on the epistle to the Galatians[9] I came across that passage in which the apostle Peter is rebuked for committing a dangerous act of deceit. I am, I admit, very upset that in that passage lying should be defended either by such a man as you or by someone else, if another person is the author, and I will continue to feel upset until what disturbs me has been removed, if that is possible. For it seems to me very dangerous to believe that the sacred writings can contain any kind of lie, in other words that those men, by whom the Bible has been given to us and written down for us, lied about anything in their writings. It is one question whether a good man should ever lie and a different question altogether whether a writer of the sacred Scriptures ought to lie; no, it is not another question, there can be no question of it at all.

Once we admit even a useful lie in that supreme authority, there will not be a single sentence left which, whenever anyone finds what is written either difficult to practise or hard to believe, cannot be explained away as a deliberately false statement on the part of the author who was lying out of a sense of duty.[10]

If the apostle Paul was lying when he rebuked the apostle Peter with the words, 'If you, although you are a Jew, live like a Gentile and not like a Jew, how can

you force the Gentiles to live like Jews?' [Gal. 2.14]
and if Paul really approved of what Peter had done
although he said and wrote that Peter had not acted
rightly, so as to mollify those who were threatening to
rebel, what shall we reply when misguided men[11] rise
up condemning marriage, as he foretold that they would
do? What shall we reply when they say that everything
which the apostle Paul said in support of the marriage
bond was a lie told not because he believed it but so
as to allay the resentment of men whose attachment to
their wives might make them rebel? To take but one
example: it might appear that there could be useful
lies even about God's glory, told with the intention of
causing half-hearted believers to be more ardent in
their love of God, but if this is so at no point in the
sacred books will the authority of pure truth stand
firm. Do we not observe what the same apostle says in
his great concern to safeguard the truth? 'If Christ
has not been raised then our preaching is in vain and
your faith is in vain. We are even guilty of
misrepresenting God because we testified of God that he
raised Christ whom he did not raise.' [1 Cor. 15.15]
If someone were to make the objection, 'Why do you find
this lie so abhorrent when what you have said, even if
it is untrue, greatly redounds to the glory of God?',
would the apostle not curse this man's madness and use
all possible words and expressions to reveal the
recesses of his heart, crying out that it is no less of
a crime, perhaps even more of one, to praise God for
things which are false than to criticise what is true?
One must therefore try to make sure that the man who is
attempting to reach an understanding of the Holy
Scriptures has a high regard for the sanctity and truth
of the sacred writings and refuses to use lies, however

expedient, to help him approve of any part of them: instead he should pass over what he does not understand and not attach more value to his own ideas than to the truth. For undoubtedly when a man makes an objection of that kind he wants people to believe him and he is trying to shake our confidence in the authority of the Holy Scriptures.

As for me, I would use whatever strength the Lord grants me to show that all those pieces of evidence which are used to prove the expediency of lying should be understood differently, so as to teach that the truth of these passages stands firm at all points. Proofs ought not to be lies, neither should they recommend lies. But I leave this to your understanding, for you will probably see this much more readily than I, once you have considered this interpretation more carefully. Your reverent spirit will compel you to this conclusion and will lead you to see that the authority of the Holy Scriptures will otherwise be undermined, in such a way that each person believes what he wants in them and does not believe what he does not wish to, once he has somehow been persuaded that those men, by whose efforts these things have been handed down to us, could have lied in their writings out of a sense of duty. Perhaps you could give us some guidelines as to when it is right to lie and when it is not, but if you do this, I beg you not to use false or dubious arguments in your explanation. I also beg you by the most true humanity of our Lord not to think me tiresome or rude. For it is no great fault - or at least not a serious one - for me to attempt to support truth, even by means of an error, if you for your part can rightly justify falsehood by means of the truth.

I would like to talk about many other things with
you since you are so candid and to discuss our
Christian studies, but no letter can satisfy this
desire of mine. I can do this more fully through the
brother whom I am pleased to have sent to you to share
in and be nourished by your conversations which are
both delightful and beneficial. And yet not even he
can perhaps take in as much of you as I would like, if
I may say so with all due respect to him. I would in
no way esteem myself more highly than him: although I
admit that I have a greater capacity for knowing you, I
see that he is becoming fuller of you and in that he
undoubtedly surpasses me. When he returns, as I hope
he soon will with the Lord's help, and when I share in
everything with which you have filled his mind, he will
not be able to fill up that part of me still empty and
greedy to know your thoughts; and so it will be that I
shall still be the more impoverished of the two and he
the richer. Anyway, this same brother is bringing some
of my writings with him; if you would be so kind as to
read them I beg you to adopt an attitude of honest and
brotherly severity. This is what I take to be the
meaning of the text: 'The good man will correct me with
mercy and rebuke me, but let not the oil of the wicked
anoint my head.' [Ps. 141.5] For I find it hard to
judge properly what I have written, because I am either
excessively diffident or more partial than I should be.
I do also sometimes see my own faults but I prefer to
be told of them by someone better in case, after having
perhaps rightly taken myself to task, I should delude
myself again and think that I have been pedantic rather
than fair in my judgement.

## NOTES

1. Augustine's friend Alypius had visited Jerome in Bethlehem in 393. In 394 he was made bishop of Thagaste. On Augustine's friendship with Alypius, see the Confesions and P. Brown's Augustine of Hippo, passim.

2. Cf. Aug. Conf. IV.6.11 [CCL 27.45]

3. Augustine is here punning on the name Profuturus which in Latin means 'he who will be of service'.

4. Origen (c. 185-c. 254) is the Greek Father to whom Augustine refers to as particularly dear to Jerome, although Jerome later changed his views at the time of the Origenist controversy (see the introduction to P. Lardet's edition of Jerome's Contra Rufinum (Apology against Rufinus). At the time when this letter was written, Jerome is known to have translated eight of Origen's homilies on Isaiah, fourteen on Jeremiah, fourteen on Ezechiel, two on the Song of Songs, as well as thirty-nine on Luke. A few years later, in 398, Jerome translated the four books of Origen's De Principiis. He had also translated works by Eusebius of Caesarea and Didymus' treatise on the Holy Spirit, of which Augustine was perhaps also aware.

5. Soon after his arrival in Bethlehem Jerome started work on a new translation into Latin of the Old Testament, based on the Septuagint text in Origen's Hexapla edition. His translation of the book of Job in this version, as well as that of the Psalms is still extant.

6. Augustine is referring to the tradition that the Hebrew Bible was originally translated into Greek by seventy (or seventy-two) translators at Alexandria in the reign of Ptolemy Philadelphus during the third century B.C. This translation became the most influential of the Greek versions and was referred to as the Septuagint, from the Latin word for seventy. Cf. Aug. dCD 18.42 [CCL 48.638].

7. Later Greek versions of the Hebrew Bible were made by Aquila, Theodotion and Symmachus; they were included, along with the Septuagint version, in the Hexapla, the elaborate edition of the Old Testament compiled by Origen.

8. For the proverbial phrase <u>mordicus tenere</u> (to hold fast with one's teeth) see Erasmus' <u>Adagia</u> I.iv.22 [CWE 31.336-7 (Toronto 1982)] in which he refers to Augustine's use of it in this letter.

9. During the years 387-9 Jerome wrote commentaries on Paul's epistles to the Philippians, the Galatians, the Ephesians and to Titus [P.L. 26].

10. Cf. Aug. De Mendac. 43 [CSEL 41.465] written in 395.

11. For example, the Manichees; cf. Aug. De Mor. Eccl. Cath. et de Mor. Manich. I.77-9 [P.L. 32.1342-4].

JEROME Ep. 103

Last year I sent you a letter[1] in the hands of
our brother Asterius the subdeacon, replying promptly
to your greeting.   I presume that you received this
letter.   Now I am asking you again, this time through
my holy brother Praesidius the deacon, firstly to keep
me in your thoughts and secondly to consider the bearer
of this letter as commended to your charge. You should
be aware that he is very dear to me:   please look after
him and support him in whatever way is necessary, not
because he is in need of anything, thanks to Christ's
goodness, but because he is very eager to win the
friendship of good men and considers himself to have
gained   the   greatest   benefit   by   forming   such
relationships.   He himself can tell you the reason for
his journey by sea to the west.

Although we are settled in our monastery, we are
tossed this way and that by fluctuating circumstances
and   we   endure   all   the   troubles   of   this   earthly
pilgrimage.[2]   But   we   trust   in   him   who   said,   'Be
confident, I have overcome the world' [John 16.33], and
believe that by means of his generosity and protection
we shall gain the victory over our enemy the devil.
Please give my regards to our holy and venerable
brother, bishop Alypius.   The holy brothers who serve
the Lord with enthusiasm in the monastery with us send
you their very best wishes.   May Christ our almighty
God keep you safe and mindful of me, my truly holy lord
and beloved bishop.

## NOTES

1. This is probably the lost letter referred to in Ep. 40.

2. It is possible that Jerome is here alluding in characteristically enigmatic terms, to the controversy between John of Jerusalem and himself. Cf. Cavallera I.193-227, Kelly pp. 195-209, Lardet's introduction to the Contra Rufinum. For the idea of this earthly life as a pilgrimage, see 2 Cor. 5.6, Aug. Enarr. in Ps. 137.12 [CCL 40.1986]; Sermo 4.9 [P.L. 38.37-8]; Sermo 346 [P.L. 39.1522-3].

AUGUSTINE Ep. 40

I am grateful to you for sending me a full-length reply to a mere greeting appended as a postscript,[1] although it was much shorter than I should have wished from a man like you because nothing you say is superfluous, however much time it takes up. And so although I am beset by numerous cares concerning other people's business and their worldly concerns, I would not easily forgive the brevity of your letter if I did not recall that it was a reply to an even shorter letter of mine. Come then, I ask you; undertake this written debate with me to prevent the physical distance between us keeping us apart, although even when we lay down our pens and are silent we are joined in the Lord by the unity of the Spirit [Eph. 4.3]. Indeed the books which you have worked hard to bring out of the granary of the Lord provide us with an almost perfect picture of you. For if the reason we do not know you is that we have not seen your actual face, then by the same argument you do not know yourself, for you do not see it either. But if you are only known to yourself because you know your own mind, then we too know it quite well through your writings and we bless the Lord for giving a man of your calibre to yourself, to me and to all the brothers who read your works.

Not long ago one of your many books[2] came into our hands. We still do not know its title, for the book itself did not provide this information on the first page, as is usually the case. The brother in whose hands it was discovered did however say it was called an obituary notice. I could believe that this

was the title you wished to ascribe to it, if we had
read in it an account of the lives and writings only of
men who are already dead, but since it mentions the
works of many people who were alive at the time it was
written and who are still living even now, I am
surprised that you gave it, or are believed to have
given it, this title.    Anyway, you have certainly
written a most useful book which meets with our
wholehearted approval.

In your commentary on the epistle of Paul the
apostle to the Galatians,(3) I found something which
causes me great concern.  If so-called white lies are
permitted in the Holy Scriptures, what authority can
these writings then have?  What statement, I ask you,
could be quoted from these Scriptures which would have
the authority to crush a wicked or a controversial
error?  For as soon as you have quoted it, if your
opponent is of a different opinion, he will say that
the text you cite is an example of the writer lying
from an honourable motive.  If it is believed and
asserted that Paul lied in the narrative at the
beginning of which he says, 'The things which I write
to you, behold before God, I do not say falsely' [Gal.
1.20], why can he not be said to be lying when he wrote
of Peter and Barnabas, 'When I saw that they did not
walk uprightly according to the truth of the Gospel'
[Gal. 2.14]?(4)  For if they were walking uprightly,
then he lied, but if he lied there, where did he speak
the truth?  Or will he be supposed to have spoken the
truth whenever he says something which the reader has
sympathy with, but when the reader comes across
anything which conflicts with his own views, will Paul
be regarded as having told a white lie?  If we allow
this rule to stand, there will be no shortage of

reasons for it being thought that the writer not only could but also should lie.  It is not necessary to discuss this question at great length, especially with you; it is enough just to state it to someone as wise and far-seeing as yourself.  Indeed I should by no means presume to attempt to enrich with my pennies that genius of yours which, by God's gift, is of pure gold; there is no one better fitted than you to correct this work.(5)  It is not for me to teach you how to understand that passage where Paul writes, 'To the Jews I became as a Jew that I might gain the Jews' [1 Cor. 9.20], and everything else which he said out of mercy and compassion, not through deceit and pretence.  For a person who nurses a sick man becomes like a sick person not by pretending to have a fever but by thinking sympathetically how he would like to be looked after if he himself were sick.  Paul was without doubt a Jew and when he became a Christian he did not give up the practices of the Jews which that people had accepted as being lawful and suitable for the times.  That is why he undertook to perform these things although he was already an apostle of Christ:  he did so in order to show that they were not harmful to those who wished to observe them in the way they had received them from their parents by means of the law even after they had come to believe in Christ.  He wanted to show that Christians ought not to set their hope of salvation in these things because the salvation which was signified by those sacraments had already come through the Lord Jesus.(6)  And so he judged that they were in no way to be imposed upon the Gentiles because such a heavy and unnecessary burden might repel them, unaccustomed as they were, from the faith.

Consequently Paul was not rebuking Peter for

observing the traditions of his fathers which could be performed without deceit or inconsistency if Peter wished (for although these customs were now superfluous they were not harmful); but he criticised him for forcing the Gentiles to live as Jews, which he could only do by himself observing these traditions as if they were still necessary for salvation even after the coming of the Lord. Truth strongly opposed this in the person of Paul the apostle and the apostle Peter knew this but he acted thus out of fear of those who were circumcised. So he was rightly rebuked, and Paul spoke the truth; otherwise, once lying is justified, Holy Scripture which has been given to promote the faith among future generations would lose its firm foundation and become completely unreliable.

It is impossible and improper to rely on letters to prove what great and complex evils would result if we admitted this; but it would be possible and appropriate - and there would be less danger of misunderstanding - if we were to discuss it in person.

And so, of the Jewish practices Paul had abandoned only what was bad: in particular the fact that being ignorant of God's righteousness and wishing to establish their own righteousness, the Jews did not submit themselves to the righteousness of God [Rom. 10.3]; and secondly the fact that after the passion and resurrection of Christ, when the sacrament of grace had been granted and revealed according to the order of Melchisedech, they still thought the old practices should be celebrated, not out of respect for the traditional ritual but because they were regarded as necessary for salvation. However, if they had never been necessary, then the martyrdom of the Maccabees in their defence[7] would have been pointless and futile.

Finally Paul rejected the practice whereby the Jews persecuted the Christian preachers of grace as if they were enemies of the law. It is these misapprehensions and faults and others like it which he says he counted as loss and dung that he might gain Christ [Phil. 3.8]; he is not referring to the observances of the law if they are kept in the traditional way, as he kept them, without any belief that they were necessary for salvation, as the Jews believed, or that they must be kept as a deceitful pretence, which is what Paul rebuked Peter for believing. If he took part in these rituals by pretending to be a Jew in order to win them over, why did he not also sacrifice with the Gentiles, putting himself outside the law as they were outside the law, so that he might win them, too?[8] Was it not because he took part in the rituals as one who was by nature a Jew and said all this not in order to pretend deceitfully to be what he was not, but because he felt that he ought to help them out of compassion, as if he himself were in danger of the same error; and so he was not acting with the cunning of a liar but with the love of one who feels compassion. Similarly in the same passage he added in more general terms, 'For the weak I became weak, that I might gain the weak' [1 Cor. 9.22], so that the conclusion which follows, 'I have become all things to all men that I might win all' [1 Cor. 9.22], might be understood to refer to the fact that he clearly pitied the weakness of each person as if it were his own. For even when he says, 'Who is weak and I am not weak?' [2 Cor. 11.29] he does not wish it to be thought that he pretends to share their weakness but rather that he sympathizes with it.

Therefore please adopt a sincere and truly Christian severity combined with love, so as to be able to correct and emend that work of yours. Sing a palinode, to use the Greek term.[9] For Christian truth is incomparably more beautiful than Helen of the Greeks.[10] Our martyrs have fought for it against this Sodom more bravely than those heroes fought for her against Troy. I am not saying this to make you regain your spiritual sight - far be it from me to think that you have lost it - but to make you notice something, for although you have healthy and keen eyes you turned them away out of some kind of deliberate disregard so as not to notice the adverse effects which would result once it was believed that a writer of the holy books could with propriety and with due reverence lie in any part of his work.

Some time ago I wrote you a letter[11] which was not delivered because the bearer[12] to whom I entrusted it never made the journey. While I was dictating this letter I remembered a remark in my earlier one which I ought to mention here: if you hold a different opinion and your opinion is better, please forgive my apprehensions. For if you hold a different opinion and your opinion is true - and unless it were true it could not be better - then my mistake, which I will not say is no fault at all but is certainly not a serious one, is intended to support the truth, if truth can rightly support falsehood in anything.[13]

With regard to what you were kind enough to write about Origen in your reply,[14] I already knew that not only in ecclesiastical writings but in all types of literature we ought to approve of and commend whatever we find there which is true and right and condemn and censure what is false and wicked. But I needed the help of your wisdom and learning and I still require you to give us an explicit account of his errors, which prove that a man of his stature departed from the true faith. In the book, too, where you listed all the ecclesiastical writers and their works you could think of,[15] it would be more useful, I think, if, after naming those whom you know to be heretical (since you decided to include these), you would also add in what ways they are unreliable. You have however omitted to mention some people and I should like to know on what grounds you did this; or if perhaps you were unwilling to overload this book by adding, to the mention of the heretics, some indication of the points on which the authority of the Catholic church has condemned them, I beg you not to regard such an undertaking as too much of a burden on your literary work. By the grace of our Lord your work has done much to encourage and assist the holy brothers in their studies in the Latin language, and I ask you for something which my brotherly love, together with my humility, requires of you, namely that (if your preoccupations allow) you should publish the false doctrines of all the heretics who have down to this day attempted to pervert the orthodoxy of the Christian faith, whether out of shamelessness or obstinacy.[16] This would help people whose other duties allow them no spare time or who are unable to read and learn so many things because they are written in a foreign language. I could persist in asking you this for a long time, if such persistence were not usually an indication that the person has little confidence in friendship. Meanwhile I commend to your kindness Paul, our brother in Christ: I can testify before God to his good reputation in our part of the world.

## NOTES

1. Both Augustine's greeting added as a postscript and Jerome's full-length reply are now lost.

2. The book which has reached Augustine is the De Viris Illustribus (Lives of Illustrious Men), the catalogue of authors written by Jerome in 392 [P.L. 23.601-720] in imitation of Suetonius' work of the same name and based on Eusebius' Church history; see the Patrologie of Altaner/Stuiber (Freiburg 1978) p. 8.

3. Jerome Comm. in Gal. 2.11 [P.L. 26.338-342] cf. Aug. Ep. 28 n. 9 above.

4. Cf. Aug. De Mendac. 43 [CSEL 41.465].

5. i.e. Jerome's commentary on the Epistle to the Galatians.

6. Cf. Aug. Cont. Faust. Manich. 19.17 [CSEL 25]; De Mendac. 8 [CSEL 41].

7. Cf. 2 Macc. 7.

8. Cf. Aug. Cont. Mendac. 26 [CSEL 41.506], a work not written until 420 but in which Augustine discusses this Scriptural passage in similar terms.

9. Augustine alludes to the palinode, or recantation, said to have been written by the Greek lyric poet Stesichorus: he had written a poem called the Helen in which he gave an account of her marriage to Menelaus; but legend (cf. Plato Phaedrus 243a) told that he was blinded for this and did not recover his sight until he recanted in a second poem, denying that Helen ever went to Troy and blaming Homer for the story.

10. Helen, whose beauty was legendary, was perhaps originally a goddess although in the Iliad and the Odyssey she is represented as the mortal wife of

Menelaus, carried off to Troy by Paris, thus providing the cause of the Trojan War.

11. i.e. Aug. Ep. 28.

12. The bearer was to have been Profuturus.

13. Augustine repeats this sentence from Ep. 28 which had not reached Jerome.

14. It is not known to which letter of Jerome Augustine is here referring.

15. Augustine refers to Jerome's work De Viris Illustribus, somewhat critical of the principle according to which Jerome compiled this survey.

16. In fact, Augustine himself, at the end of his life, produced a work De Haeresibus, giving a brief description of 88 heresies [CCL 46].

AUGUSTINE Ep. 67

I was told that my letter[1] had reached you but I do not blame you at all for the fact that I have not yet deserved an answer; no doubt something has prevented it. I realise therefore that I must rather pray to the Lord that he should grant you the opportunity to send your reply, as well as the will to reply - for he has already granted you the opportunity to reply since you were easily able to do it when you wanted.

I was actually in doubt whether to believe another thing which was reported to me but I ought not to be in doubt whether to mention it to you. This is it, in brief: I was told that it had been hinted to you - I do not know by which of the brothers - that I had written a book against you and sent it to Rome. Please realise that this is not true. I swear to you before God that I did not do such a thing.[2] But if it happens that certain passages are found in some of my writings expressing opinions which conflict with yours, I think you ought to realise that they were not directed against you but that I wrote what I believed to be true; or if you cannot see that, then you must believe it. Indeed I say this to show you that I am not only very prepared to receive in a brotherly spirit your contrary views (should there be anything in my writings which disturbs you), but that I even beg and entreat you to do this, for I will take pleasure in my own correction and in your kindness.

If only it were possible, even if we could not live together, at least to have you close at hand and to enjoy frequent and pleasant conversations with you in the Lord! But since this has not been granted, I ask you to make every effort to preserve our unity in Christ, (for in him we are as united as we can be) and even to increase and perfect that unity; and please do not neglect to reply to my letters, even if only occasionally. Give my regards to your holy brother Paulinianus[3] and to all the brothers who rejoice in the Lord with you and in you. Remember me and I pray that the Lord may grant every holy desire of yours, my beloved master and my longed for and respected brother in Christ.

## NOTES

1. Probably Augustine's Ep. 40

2. Augustine justifiably denies that he has sent a book attacking Jerome to Rome; he does not realise that the rumour refers to his Ep. 40 which reached Rome unbeknown to its author.

3. Paulinianus was Jerome's younger brother; the two brothers lived together from about 385. Cf. Jer. Ep. 82.8.

JEROME Ep. 102

Our blessed son Asterius the subdeacon was about to
set off when your letter[1] arrived, in which you
assure me that you did not send a book to Rome directed
against me. I had heard nothing about this, but our
brother Sisinnius the deacon brought me copies of a
letter[2] apparently addressed to me, in which you urge
me to sing a palinode with regard to a certain chapter
written by the apostle Paul and to imitate Stesichorus
who vacillated between abusing and praising Helen and
who by praising her regained the sight which he had
lost by criticising her. I admit frankly to you that
although the style and the arguments seemed to me to be
yours, I did not think that I should put unquestioning
faith in mere copies of a letter, in case my reply
should offend you and you should justifiably complain
that I ought to have ascertained that it was your work
before replying to it. Another reason for my delay in
replying has been the long illness of the blessed and
venerable Paula.[3] While I was spending long periods
tending the patient, I almost forgot your letter or
rather the letter which someone had written in your
name, for I remembered that verse, 'A tale out of time
is like music in mourning'.[4] If the letter is yours,
please inform me of it openly or send a more accurate
copy so that our discussions of Scripture may be
completely devoid of any anger or bitterness and we may
either correct our mistakes or prove to each other that
the other's criticism was unfounded.

Far be it from me to dare to attack anything in
your writings; I have enough to do to defend my own
work without criticising that of others. However, you

are well aware that each person is fully persuaded of
his own beliefs and that it is a mark of childish
boastfulness - the sort of behaviour that boys used to
indulge in - to seek fame for oneself by attacking
illustrious men. I am not so foolish as to be offended
if your interpretations differ from mine; neither
should you feel offended if I hold a different opinion.
What is truly reprehensible behaviour between friends
is, as Persius writes, to look carefully at the bag
carried by others but to disregard our own.[5] It
remains for you to love one who loves you and not,
young man as you are, to challenge an old man to a
fight in the field of Scripture. My time is spent and
I have run the course to the best of my ability. Now
while you are still running and covering great
distances, I deserve some rest. However, if I may say
so with respect, I do not wish people to think that you
are the only one who can quote from the poets:
remember Dares and Entellus[6] and the popular proverb
about the tired ox treading with a heavier step.[7] It
is with sadness that I have dictated these words. I
wish that I might be thought worthy to embrace you and
to converse with you, so that each of us might learn
and teach something.

Calpurnius, surnamed Lanarius,[8] has with his
usual effrontery sent me his abusive writings. I
understand that through his efforts they have reached
Africa. I have written a brief and partial reply to
them and have sent you a copy of this work;[9] I shall
send a more comprehensive reply at the first possible
opportunity. In this book I have been careful not to
say anything which might discredit Christians but only
to confute the lies and delusions of this ignorant
fool. Remember me, holy and venerable father. See how

much I love you in that even when provoked I was unwilling to reply and I refused to believe writings to be yours which I would strongly criticise if they were someone else's. The brother we share[10] greets you respectfully.

## NOTES

1. Augustine's Ep. 67.

2. Aug. Ep. 40

3. Paula was the aristocratic widow who had become Jerome's friend and pupil at Rome. When he left for Bethlehem in 385, Paula acompanied him together with her daughter Eustochium and there they founded a monastery and a convent. The illness of which Jerome writes here occurred some two years before Paula's death in 404.

4. Sirach 22.6.

5. Persius Sat. 4.24.

6. See Virgil Aen. 5.368-484 for the account of the boxing match between Dares and Entellus, in which the veteran Entellus, against the odds, is aroused to such a point that he finally emerges victorious over the younger champion who had been confident of winning. Jerome warns Augustine that he might suffer the same fate as Dares if he challenges the veteran Jerome.

7. See Erasmus' Adagia I.1.47 [CWE 31 p. 97] for an explanation of this proverbial phrase. 'St. Jerome, with great elegance, makes use of this adage when writing to St. Augustine, wishing to dissuade him, being still young, from challenging an older man. The point is that those who are already tired because of their age are slower to be provoked to battle but they are the ones who are fiercer and more pressing when that elderly courage of theirs, aroused, grows hot again.'

8. The name Lanarius probably refers to Jerome's one-time friend Rufinus, for whom Jerome produced a number of disparaging or cruel nicknames (e.g. scorpion, serpent, Grunnius) after the breakdown of their friendship as a result of the Origenist controversy. For the connection between Rufinus and the character referred to in Sallust's Histories, see Schmid p. 40; for the use of the name Calpurnius for Rufinus, cf. Jer. Apol. cont. Ruf. I.30 [CCL 79 p. 29].

9. This reply to Rufinus' abuse was probably Jerome's letter to Rufinus which forms the third book of his Apology against Rufinus, written some time after the first two books and defending himself against the charges made in Rufinus' Apology against him and in a (lost) letter to Jerome.

10. If we accept the emendation (communis) of Cavallera [I p. 300 n. 1] as against the reading (Communis) of Hilberg [CSEL 55 p. 236] and Goldbacher [CSEL 34 p. 243], Jerome is probably referring to his brother Paulinianus.

AUGUSTINE Ep. 71

Since I began to write to you and to long for your letters, I have never had a better opportunity of sending my letter to you than now when it is being conveyed by that most faithful servant and minister of God, our son the deacon Cyprian, who is so very dear to me. Through him I definitely hope to receive a letter from you - there is nothing I hope for with greater confidence. For the son whom I have just mentioned will lack neither determination in demanding a reply nor the charm to deserve one, nor diligence in looking after it nor eagerness in bearing it nor reliability in delivering it. If, then, I am in any way worthy, may the Lord assist you and favour your heart and my wishes, so that no greater will may obstruct this brotherly desire.

As I have already sent you two letters[1] without receiving any reply to them, I decided to send the same ones again, assuming that they did not reach you. But if you did receive them and it was perhaps your letters instead which did not succeed in reaching me, please send once again exactly those letters which you have already sent, if you happen to have kept copies of them. If not, dictate them again for me to read and do not feel it is too much trouble to reply to this one, for I have been waiting a long time. My first letter[2] to you I prepared while I was still only a priest, intending it to be sent in the hands of Profuturus, one of our brothers who later became a fellow-bishop of ours and has now departed this life; even then he was unable to convey the letter, because at the exact time that he was planning to set out he was detained by the burden of the episcopate and died

shortly afterwards. I have decided to send this letter
also to you now so that you may know how long I have
been ardently longing for a conversation with you and
the torment I suffer because of the great distance
separating me from your physical presence, which would
allow my mind to come close to yours, my dearest
brother whom I honour among the members of the Lord.

But in this letter I should add what I only learned
at a later date, namely that you had translated the
book of Job from the Hebrew although we already have a
translation into Latin of that prophet which you made
from the Greek text;[3] in the first version you used
asterisks to mark those passages which are found in the
Hebrew text but are missing from the Greek, and
obelisks to indicate the passages to be found in the
Greek text but not in the Hebrew; you have done this
with such amazing thoroughness that in certain places
each individual word is marked by an asterisk informing
the reader that these words are in the Hebrew text but
not in the Greek. However, in this later version
translated from the Hebrew, there is not the same
precision in noting the words and it is somewhat
confusing to the reader who wonders why asterisks were
inserted in the first version, great care being taken
to mark even the smallest grammatical particles which
were absent from the Greek text but present in the
Hebrew; or why in this later version, made from the
Hebrew texts, less care was taken in making sure that
these same particles were to be found in their proper
places. I wanted to give some example of this, but at
the moment I am without a manuscript of the version
made from the Hebrew. But since your intellect is so
superior to mine, you will understand well, I am sure,
not only what I have said, but even what I want to say,

and will be able to explain to me the reasons for what you did.

To be honest, I would prefer you to translate the canonical books of Scripture for us from the Greek text which is known as the Septuagint. I feel that many problems would arise if your translation began to be read regularly in many churches, because the Latin churches would be out of step with the Greek ones, especially as anyone who puts forward objections will easily be proved wrong when the Greek text is produced, for Greek is a language almost universally known. If, however, someone were to object to some unusual expression in the version translated from the Hebrew and were to allege that it is wrong, it would be almost impossible to get hold of the Hebrew texts to use in defence of the point to which he objected. But even if it were possible, who would allow so many Latin and Greek authorities to be condemned? In addition, if Hebrew scholars were consulted, they might give a different answer and so you might appear indispensable as the only one who could prove them wrong - but I would be amazed if you could find anyone to arbitrate between you.

To take an example: when one of our fellow bishops arranged for your translation to be read in a church in his diocese, they came across a word in your version of the prophet Jonah which you had rendered very differently from the translation with which they were familiar[4] and which, having been read by so many generations, was ingrained in their memories. A great uproar ensued in the congregation, especially among the Greeks who criticised the text and passionately denounced it as wrong, and the bishop (the incident took place in the city of Oea) was compelled to ask the

Jews to give evidence. Whether out of ignorance or
spite, they replied that this word did occur in the
Hebrew manuscripts in exactly the same form as in the
Greek and Latin versions. In short, the man was forced
to correct the passage in your version as if it were
inaccurate since he did not want this crisis to leave
him without a congregation. This makes even us suspect
that you, too, can be mistaken occasionally. Just
think what would happen in the case of writings which
cannot be corrected by comparing the testimony of
languages still in daily use!

Nevertheless we give thanks to God in no small
measure for your work in translating the Gospels from
the Greek; when we compared it with the Greek
Scriptures we found hardly anything to object to in the
whole work.[5] And if anyone were to persist in his
support of false readings of the old version, he would
easily be convinced or confuted if the manuscripts were
produced and a comparison made. But if, as is very
occasionally the case, there is something which
justifiably offends, would anyone be so harsh as not to
show some indulgence towards such a useful work which
cannot be praised highly enough? Would you be so kind
as to explain what you believe to be the reason why, in
many cases, the authority of the Hebrew manuscripts
differs from that of the Greek text, known as the
Septuagint? For this text is of great importance,
seeing that it was so widely diffused and was used by
the apostles[6] - a fact which is proved not only by
the text itself but which I remember you also
confirmed. You would thus be doing a great service if
you were to make an accurate Latin translation of the
Greek version of Scripture produced by the Seventy, for
the Greek text contains so many divergent readings in

different manuscripts that it is almost intolerable: when one always suspects that a different reading might be found in the Greek text, one hesitates to use any quotations or proofs from it.

I thought this letter was going to be a short one but it has somehow been as enjoyable to continue with it as if I were talking with you. But I beg you in the Lord's name not to be reluctant to reply to all my queries and to give me, as far as is possible, the pleasure of your company.

## NOTES

1. i.e. Ep. 28 and Ep. 40.

2. Augustine's Ep. 28.

3. Jerome's translation of the book of Job made from the Hebrew rather than from the Greek was probably completed in 393 (see Jerome's letter to Pammachius, Ep. 49.4). Cf. Aug. Ep. 28 n. 5 above.

4. i.e. Jonah 4.6-10; see Jerome's commentary on Jonah, edited by P. Antin (Sources Chrétiennes 43, Paris 1956). The Latin version with which the congregation at Oea were familiar was probably the so-called Vetus Latina.

5. This statement of Augustine's implies that he had some knowledge of Greek, as would be expected considering his education. On the vexed question of the extent of his familiarity with Greek, see Brown p. 271 with n. 2 and Bonner pp. 394-5.

6. Although Jerome and Augustine did not agree about the status of the Septuagint translation, they both supported their views by referring to apostolic authority; cf. Jer. Apol. cont. Ruf. II.34 [CCL 79.71].

JEROME Ep. 105

    You send me one letter after another and
continually demand a  reply to a certain letter of
yours,[1] a copy of which, without your signature, was
brought to me by brother Sisinnius the deacon, as I
have already told you in a letter.[2]  You say[3] that
you first gave this letter to brother Profuturus to
deliver and then to someone else but that in the
meantime Profuturus was prevented from undertaking the
journey by being ordained bishop and he then passed
away suddenly, while the other man,[4] whose name you
do not mention, fearing the dangers involved in a sea
voyage, changed his mind about his journey. If this is
so, I am completely at a loss to explain how that
letter can be rumoured to be in the possession of a
number of people at Rome and in Italy and how I alone,
the only one to whom it was addressed, did not receive
it, especially since this brother Sisinnius said that
he had found this letter among other exegetical works
of yours, not in Africa, not in your possession, but on
an island in the Adriatic about five years ago!

    Friendship ought to be free from all suspicion and
one should be able to talk to a friend as to a second
self.  Some of my close friends, vessels of Christ,
many of whom live at Jerusalem and in the holy places,
suggested to me that you had not acted with complete
frankness in doing this, but had done so in a desire
for praise and fame and popularity, seeking to increase
your reputation at my expense and to make people see
that when you challenge me, I am afraid, and that when
you, a man of learning, write to me, I keep quiet like

an ignorant fool, now that someone has been found who
can put a stop to my chatter. However, I was unwilling
to reply to you - let me be honest - first of all
because I did not believe that the letter nor the
honey-coated sword (to use a proverbial expression)[5]
was yours; secondly because I was anxious not to appear
impertinent in my reply to a bishop of my own communion
and critical of something in the letter of someone who
was criticising me, especially since I considered some
of its statements to be heretical.

And then I was afraid that you might have reason to
remonstrate with me, saying, 'What! If you saw my
letter and found the signature to be in a familiar
hand, how could you injure a friend so thoughtlessly
and base your abuse of me on another persons's spite?'
And so, as I have already said in an earlier letter,[6]
either send me the same letter signed by your own hand
or cease to provoke an old man who is cowering in his
little cell. If you wish to show off or practise your
erudition, then find some eloquent and well-born young
men: there are said to be a great number of them at
Rome, who could - and would be audacious enough to -
meet you and engage in a discussion of Scripture with a
bishop on equal terms. I was once an active soldier
but now I have been pensioned off: it is for me to
praise your victories and those of other men rather
than to enter the fray again myself, physically
exhausted as I am. Otherwise, if you persist in
demanding a reply, I will have to remind you of the
story of how Quintus Maximus' patience got the better
of Hannibal despite the latter's youthful self-
confidence.[7]

Time bears all away, even memory. I remember that
as a boy I often used to spend the long summer days

singing.    Now  I  have  forgotten  all  those  songs,  and
Moeris  is  even  losing  his  voice.[8]

Or  to  take  an  example  from  holy  Scripture,  when
Barzillai  the  Gileadite  handed  over  all  King  David's
gifts  and  charms  to  his  young  son,  he  made  it  clear
that  old  men  ought  not  to  seek  such  things  nor  to
accept  them  when  offered.[9]

You  swear  that  you  did  not  write  a  letter  directed
against  me  and  did  not  send  to  Rome  something  you  had
not  written,  but  you  say  that  if  anything  should  by
chance  be  discovered  in  your  writings  which  is  at
variance  with  my  views,  I  should  not  take  offence  since
you  were  only  writing  what  you  believed  to  be  true.[10]
I  beg  you  to  listen  to  me  patiently.    You  did  not  write
that  book:    why  then  was  a  work  brought  to  me  by  others
containing  your  criticisms  of  me?    Why  is  a  letter  of
yours,  which  you  did  not  write,  circulating  throughout
Italy?    Why  do  you  demand  a  reply  from  me  to  a  letter
which  you  say  you  did  not  write?    I  am  not  so  stupid  as
to  take  offence  because  you  hold  a  different  opinion
from  me,  but  if  you  attack  what  I  say  in  single  combat
and  demand  a  reason  for  what  I  write  and  force  me  to
change  what  I  have  written,  challenging  me  to  sing  a
palinode  and  recover  my  eyesight,  then  you  are  harming
our  friendship  and  violating  the  conventions  which
govern  such  relationships.    I  am  writing  this  so  that
we  should  not  seem  to  be  fighting  in  a  childish  manner
or  provide  our  admirers  or  critics  with  material  for
dispute.    I  wish  to  love  you  in  a  sincere  and  Christian
manner  and  do  not  want  my  thoughts  to  contain  anything
which  is  not  in  harmony  with  what  I  say.    It  is  not
right  that  I,  who  have  spent  the  whole  time  from  my
earliest  youth  until  now  sweating  over  my  work  in  this
little  monastery  together  with  the  holy  brothers,

should venture to write anything against a bishop of my communion and indeed, that very bishop whom I began to love before I got to know him, who solicited my friendship first and who I was glad to hear was following in my footsteps in the study of Scripture. And so you must either deny that the book is yours if it happens not to be and cease to demand a reply to something which you did not write, or if it is yours, admit it openly so that if I write anything in my own defence, the responsibility will be with you who issued the challenge and not with me, who was forced to reply.

You add also that you are prepared to accept it in a spirit of brotherly love, should anything offend me in your writings or should I wish to correct anything; you also say that you would not only rejoice in such a show of good will towards you on my part but you even beg me to do so.(11) I shall tell you again what I feel. You are provoking an old man, you are rousing one who is silent and you give the impression that you are showing off your learning. But it is not for someone of my age to be considered unkind towards a person whom I ought rather to encourage. If wicked men find things even in the Gospels or in the books of the prophets which they wish to criticise, are you surprised if some points in your writings appear to be wide of the mark - especially in your exposition of Scripture which is full of difficulties? I am not saying this because I think that anything in your works deserves to be criticised; I have never read them with attention and we do not have many copies of them, apart from your Soliloquies and some of your commentaries on the Psalms.(12) If I were willing to examine them closely, I could show that they were at variance - I will not say with my own interpretations, but with those of earlier Greek writers. Farewell, my dearest friend, you who are a son to me in years but a father in merit. I beg you, please make sure that I am the first to read whatever you write to me.

## NOTES

1. i.e. Aug. Ep. 40.

2. Jer. Ep. 102.

3. Jerome is referring to Augustine's Ep. 71.

4. This unknown person is not mentioned in any of Augustine's extant letters.

5. For the proverbial phrase litum melle gladium, see Otto p. 218.

6. Jer. Ep. 102.1.

7. An account of this episode between Hannibal and Fabius Cunctator (to whom Jerome refers as Quintus Maximus) is found in Livy 22.12-18.

8. Virgil Ecl. 8.51-4.

9. For the story of the aged Barzillai's encounter with David see 2 Sam. 19.31-40.

10. Jerome refers to what Augustine wrote in his Ep. 67.

11. Aug. Ep. 67.

12. Augustine had written his Soliloquies [P.L. 32] at Cassiciacum in 386; he was engaged in writing the Enarrationes in Psalmos for a long period - the first part, comprising Pss. 1-32 [CCL 38], had been produced by 392, while the last one he wrote, on Ps. 118, was not completed until 418.

AUGUSTINE Ep. 73

I believe that before this letter reaches you, you
will have received the one[1] which I sent with our son
Cyprian, the deacon and servant of God. This will have
made you realise that it definitely was my letter,[2] a
copy of which you said reached you and which I now
think was the reason why I began to be beaten and
harrassed by your reply, like the over-confident Dares
attacked by Entellus' powerful and savage blows.[3]
This letter is now a reply to the one[4] you deigned to
send me in the hands of our holy son Asterius, in which
I found many indications of your benevolent and loving
feelings towards me, but also some signs that I had
offended you in some way. As I was reading I felt at
one moment delighted but at the next moment dumbfounded
and amazed, most of all by the fact that after saying
that you did not think you should rashly lend credence
to copies of my letter (in case I might perhaps
justifiably complain that I had been injured by your
reply because you ought only to have replied once you
had proved that the contents were mine), you then went
on to order me to write and tell you openly whether the
letter is mine or to send authenticated copies so that
we might continue our discussions about Scripture
without any anger or bitterness. But how can we
continue with this discussion without bitterness if you
are prepared to injure me? Or even if you are not, how
would I be justified, if you had not injured me, in
complaining that you had attacked me, saying that you
ought to have proved that the contents were mine before

replying, or rather, before attacking me? For if you had not attacked me in your reply, I could not justifiably complain. Accordingly, since you replied to my letter in such a way as to cause me offence, what room is left to us for continuing our Scriptural discussions without any bitterness? Far be it from me to take offence if you should wish - and be able - to prove conclusively to me that you have interpreted this problematic passage from the apostle's letter or any other passage in the Holy Scriptures more accurately than me. No, indeed, I would rather be grateful to you and consider it to be to my advantage if I were instructed by such a teacher as you or corrected by such a critic as you.

Moreover, my dearest brother, unless you felt offended by my writings, you would not think that I could feel offended by your reply. For I would never have believed it of you, that without considering yourself offended, you would reply in such a way as to offend me. Or if this was not your intention when you replied, you still thought me foolish enough to take offence, and you certainly have offended me by thinking this of me. You should not have jumped to the conclusion that I was that kind of person, seeing that you were unwilling lightly to put faith in copies of my letter, even though you recognised my style. If you rightly recognised that I would be justified in complaining if you jumped to the conclusion that the letter was mine when it was not, would I not be much more justified in complaining that you had rashly formed an estimate of me which was contradicted by your own experience? You should then by no means make the mistake of thinking me so foolish that I could be offended by your reply even when, in replying, you had no intention of injuring me.

The only conclusion is that you would be prepared to injure me in your reply if it was proved to you beyond doubt that the letter was mine. But as I do not believe that you think that I should be attacked without just cause, it remains for me to admit my wrong in first attacking you in that letter[5] which I cannot deny was mine. Why should I try to swim against the current? Why not beg you to forgive me instead? I beseech you, therefore, by Christ's mercy, to forgive me if I have offended you and not to retaliate by attacking me in return. I would however be offended if you did not inform me of any error of mine which you might perhaps discover in anything I do or say. But if you rebuke me for things which are not reprehensible, you are hurting yourself more than me because it is not compatible with your manner of living and your holy ideals for you to do this with the intention of hurting me, out of ill-will blaming me for something which you know in all honesty that I am not to be blamed for. Consequently either you should rebuke me out of the kindness of your heart, even if I have no fault which you think deserves to be criticised (for it is possible that you do not see things as they really are, but the important thing is that all your actions should be inspired by love),[6] - I would be most grateful to be given a friendly rebuke even if what could justly be defended did not deserve criticism; or I would acknowledge both your kindness and my fault and - as far as the Lord grants it to me - I shall be found grateful for the former and stand corrected as to the latter. Why should I fear your words (which may be harsh but are certainly salutary) as if they were Entellus' boxing gloves? He was beaten up, not cured and was therefore defeated, not healed. But if I calmly accept your healing rebuke, I will suffer no pain; and if, due to a certain weakness which is either common to human nature or peculiar to myself, I do feel a little upset when I am rebuked even for a good reason, it is still better for a tumour on the head to be cured though the treatment is painful, than for it to be left and thus never to heal. For this was clearly seen by the person who said that the censure of enemies is often more useful than friends who are afraid to criticise;[7] when our enemies find fault with us they sometimes speak the truth and we can correct our behaviour, while our friends may show less frankness than they should because they are afraid to embitter the sweetness of friendship. For this reason even if you have the impression that you are an ox, physically exhausted perhaps by old age but not in your mental energy - for you can still work hard and profitably on the Lord's threshing floor - here I am: if I have said anything amiss, tread more firmly. The weight of your old age should not trouble me, as long as the chaff of my fault is threshed out.

It is with a deep sigh of longing that I read and recall to mind what you wrote right at the end of your letter: 'I wish that I might deserve to embrace you and converse with you so that each of us might learn and teach something.'[8] But I say, 'If only we could at least live closer to each other so that, even if conversation were impossible, our letters could be more frequent.' As it is, so great is the distance separating us and preventing us from any kind of access to each other through the eye and ear that I remember that I wrote to you in my youth about the apostle's words to the Galatians and look! now I am already an

old man but I have not yet been rewarded with a reply
from you. Meanwhile copies of my letter reached you by
some strange accident earlier than the letter itself,
despite the care I took in sending it. For the man who
took it in the first place did not deliver it to you
nor did he return it to me. The learning you display
in that letter of yours which did manage to reach me is
so impressive that I would give up all my studies if it
meant that I could be always at your side. But as this
is impossible, I am considering sending you one of our
sons in the Lord to be educated, if indeed I deserve a
reply from you on this matter. For I am not, and
cannot be, as learned in the Holy Scriptures as I see
you are; if I do have some ability in this field, I
devote it in one way or another to the people of God.
But because of my duties as a bishop it is absolutely
impossible for me to spend more time on my studies than
on teaching my congregation.[9]

I was not aware that certain writings attacking
your reputation had reached Africa, but we did receive
what you deigned to send in reply to those insults.[10]
When I read it through, I admit that I was very upset
that such terrible discord should have arisen between
two such dear and intimate people, joined by a bond of
friendship which was well-known throughout almost all
the churches. It is quite clear from that work of
yours that you exercised considerable self-restraint
and held back the shafts of your resentment to stop
yourself returning insult for insult. And if I was
grief-stricken and petrified with fear when I read that
one, what effect would the things which he wrote
against you[11] have on me, should they happen to fall
into my hands! How terrible for the world that there
are things that make people lose their faith.[12] Now

it is happening - witness the fulfilment of what truth foretold: 'Such will be the spread of evil that many people's love will grow cold.' [Matt. 24.12] For what loyal hearts can now safely return each other's affection? Into whose heart can love throw itself wholeheartedly without any risk? What friend is not to be feared as a potential enemy, if such a lamentable rift can occur between Jerome and Rufinus? What a wretched and distressing state of affairs! How unreliable is our knowledge of our present friends' feelings if we cannot know anything about our future friends! But why should I think that it must be a source of grief that one person is ignorant of what may happen to someone else, when no man can know even what will become of himself? He hardly knows what he is like now; what he will be like later on, he has no idea. If the pure and blessed angels possess a knowledge not only of what each one is, but can also see what he will be like, I do not understand how the devil could ever have been happy, even when he was still a good angel, if he was able to foresee his own sin and eternal punishment.(13) I would like to know your views on the subject, if indeed you consider it a question worth answering.

Just look what the land and sea are doing keeping us physically apart! If I were this letter of mine which you are now reading, you could tell me what I wish to know, but as it is, when will you write back? When will you send the letter? When will it arrive? When shall I receive it? But since our correspondence cannot reach its destination as quickly as we would like, we must bear the delays with as much patience as possible, as long as it arrives some time. And so I return to those words in your letter which were so gentle and full of holy longing; I shall adopt them and make them my own: I wish that I might deserve to embrace you and converse with you so that each of us might learn and teach something[14] - if it is at all possible for me to teach you anything.

I am delighted and reinvigorated by these words which are now mine as much as yours, and to some extent consoled while this longing which we both experience remains unfulfilled, not yet having attained what it desires; but I still feel deeply pained when I consider that the worm of bitterness has crept between you and Rufinus. And yet God granted you in large measure that very thing which we both desired, namely that you might together, in great intimacy and unity, taste the honey of the Holy Scriptures. Surely everyone everywhere must fear this worm at all times, seeing that it came between you two, men of mature age, living in the word of the Lord, at a time when you were following the Lord untrammelled by the burdens of this world, living together in that country[15] in which the Lord, when he walked with human feet, said, 'My peace I give you, my peace I leave with you.' [John 14.27] Man's life on earth is certainly a time of trial.[16] Alas that I am unable to find you both together somewhere! If I could, I might perhaps, in my concern and in my feelings of pain and fear, throw myself at your feet and weep to the limit of my strength; I would beg you, to the limit of my love, not to publish in writing statements about each other which might make it difficult for you to be friends again, because they cannot be deleted should you become reconciled or which you might fear to read once you had made up your quarrel, in case they should make you quarrel again. I beg each of you now to do this for his own sake, for

each other's sake and for the sake of all other people,
especially the weak for whom Christ died, who are
watching you in the theatre of this life, so to speak,
and for whom the outcome is of crucial importance.

But I must admit that nothing disturbed me more
with regard to this case than when I read certain
things in your letter which reveal your resentment
towards me: not so much the bits about Entellus and
the tired ox, where you seem to me to be making a good-
humoured joke rather than angry threats; I am more
worried by what you appear to have written in all
seriousness and which I mentioned earlier in the letter
(when I perhaps said more than I ought to have but not
more than my fear prompted me to.) I am referring to
the passage where you say,' In case you should perhaps
justifiably complain that you have been attacked.'[17]
I beg you that if possible we should discuss things in
such a way that our hearts can be nourished without the
bitterness of discord. If I am unable to mention what
I think needs to be corrected in your writings and you
in mine, without there being a suspicion of envy or
some injury to our friendship, we had better give up
these things and think only of what is conducive to our
life and health. It does not matter if we pursue
learning, which makes men conceited, with less
persistence as long as love, which edifies, is not
injured.[18] I recognise that I am a long way from
that perfection of which it is written, 'If a man does
not offend in word, then he is perfect' [James 3.2],
but I think that through God's mercy I can easily beg
you to forgive me if I have offended you in any way.
You ought to tell me so openly, so that when I hear
you, you might benefit your brother; you ought not to
allow me to continue in error just because the great

distance between our countries prevents you informing me in person. As regards those things which we seek to know, if I am convinced or if I believe or think that I possess the truth on some subject about which you hold a different opinion, I shall attempt to assert it without attacking you, as far as the Lord allows. But as regards your resentment, when I perceive that I have offended you, I shall simply beg you to forgive me.

I certainly do not think that you could have got angry unless I said something which I ought not to have or did not say it in the way I ought to have, for it is not surprising that we know each other less well than we are known to our closest and most intimate friends. I admit that I can easily abandon myself to their love, especially when I am worn out by the scandals of this world and I can rest in their love, free from cares and convinced that God is there; I can safely cast myself on him and rest safely in him. In my freedom from anxiety I have absolutely no fear of that uncertainty of the future, inherent in man's weakness, which I was lamenting earlier in the letter. When I feel that a man is burning with Christian love which has made him a loyal friend, whatever plans or thoughts of mine which I entrust to him, I know that I am entrusting them not to a mere man but to God, in whom my friend remains so as to be what he is; for God is love and anyone who remains in love remains in God and God in him [1 John 4.16]. If he has abandoned God, it must necessarily cause as much pain as his remaining there would cause joy.

But someone who turns from an intimate friend into an enemy can think up for himself something to put forward in all cunning, but he should not discover facts which he might reveal when angry. However, each person readily achieves this not by concealing what he has done but by not doing what he would want to hide. By God's mercy it is granted to good and devout people to live free and secure among potential enemies without betraying another person's sins which have been confided to them and without themselves committing any sins which they would be afraid to have revealed. When a spiteful person invents something untrue, it is either given no credence whatsoever or the reputation alone is discredited while the soul's chance of salvation remains undamaged; but when an evil deed is committed, the enemy is within, even if it is not divulged by any friend's gossip or quarrel. That is why any sensible person would acknowledge how patiently, with your conscience to console you, you now bear the unbelievable hostility of someone who was once your dearest and closest friend and how you consider both what he utters and what he is perhaps believed by some to utter, to belong to the weapons for the left hand which are used no less than those on the right hand in the fight against the devil.[19] However I would prefer him somehow to be more moderate, so that you would not need to be armed like that. It is a great source of sadness and amazement that such a friendship has turned into such enmity, but our joy will be all the greater when you return to your former intimacy after this period of hostility.

NOTES

1. i.e. Aug. Ep. 71.

2. Aug. Ep. 40.

3. Cf. Jer. Ep. 102 n. 6.

4. Jer. Ep. 102.

5. Aug. Ep. 40.

6. I have accepted the emendation made by Vaccari.

7. Cf. Cic. Lael. 24.90.

8. Jer. Ep. 102.2.

9. The text at this point is problematic. Goldbacher [CSEL 34. 269] reads, 'vacare autem studiosis diligentius, quam populi audiunt, instruendis propter ecclesiaticas occupationes omnino non possum,' but I base my translation on the following emended version, 'vacare autem studiis diligentius quam populi audiunt(?) instruendi, propter ecclesiasticas occupationes omnino non possum.'

10. i.e. Jer. Apol. cont. Ruf. III [CCL 79].

11. Rufinus had first sent his Apology against Jerome and later a letter (no longer extant), both of which provoked a savage reply from Jerome. See Cavallera I.

12. Cf. Matt. 18.7.

13. Cf. Aug. dCD 9.22 [CCL 47.268-9].

14. Jer. Ep. 102.2.

15. Both Jerome and Rufinus had settled in the Holy Land and lived there for many years, Jerome from the year 386 in Bethlehem while Rufinus spent about twenty years, from the late 370's, on the Mount of Olives.

16. Cf. Job 7.1.

17. Jer. Ep. 102.1.

18. Cf. 1 Cor. 8.1.
19. Cf. 2 Cor. 6.7.

JEROME Ep. 112


I received three of your letters,[1] or rather three short books, at the same time: they were brought to me by the deacon Cyprian and they all contain various questions (as you call them) or criticisms (as I consider them) referring to my minor writings. If I were to answer them my reply would need to be as long as a book, but I will try, as far as I can, not to exceed the proper limits of a letter, though rather a lengthy one, and not to keep my brother waiting for he is in a hurry. He asked me for a reply only three days before his planned date of departure, and so I am forced to blurt these things out without any semblance of order or forethought, as it were in the midst of battle, and to reply with a confused account, not with the consideration which someone writing would give to his letter, but with the hastiness typical of someone dictating; in the same way an unexpected battle throws even the bravest soldiers into confusion and forces them to flee before they can take up arms.

However, our armour is Christ as well as the command of the apostle who wrote to the Ephesians, 'Take the whole armour of God so that you may be able to withstand on the evil day' [Eph. 6.13], and a little further on, 'Stand firm, having righteousness and put on your feet the equipment of the gospel of peace; above all take the shield of faith with which you can quench all the flaming darts of the evil one and take the helmet of salvation and the sword of the spirit which is the word of God.' [Eph. 6.14-17] Armed with these weapons, King David once went out to battle.[2] He took five smooth stones out of the stream to show

that his thoughts contained nothing bitter or filthy
even amid the whirlpool of this world, as he drank from
the stream on the way; and then with head held high, he
chopped off the head of the arrogant Goliath with the
Philistine's own sword - this was particularly
significant - and struck the blasphemer on the forehead
- wounding him on that part of the body where also
Uzziah was struck with leprosy for usurping the duties
of the priesthood.[3]  The blessed David gloried in the
Lord, saying, 'The light of your countenance has shined
upon us.' [Ps. 4.6/7]  Let us therefore also say,'My
heart is ready, O God, my heart is ready.  I shall sing
and chant in my glory.  Arise, o harp and lyre, I will
awake at dawn,' [Ps. 56.8-9 (57.7-8); Ps. 107.2-3
(108.1-2)] so that in us may be fulfilled the words of
psalm 80, 'Open your mouth and I will fill it,' [Ps.
80.11 (81.10)] and of psalm 67, 'The Lord will give the
word to those who bring the good news with great
strength.' [Ps. 67.12 (68.11)]

I do not hesitate to beg you that truth may also
prevail in our discussions.  You do not seek your own
glory but that of Christ and when you win the argument,
then I too will be the winner if I perceive my mistake,
and conversely, if I get the better of you, then you
will also be the winner. Children ought not to lay up
treasures for their parents but rather parents for
their children[4] and in the book of Chronicles[5] we
read that the sons of Israel went out to battle with
thoughts of peace and even amidst the swords, the
shedding of blood and the scattered corpses, they were
not intent on their own victory but on that of peace.

I shall try to reply to all your questions and
solve the many problems succinctly, if Christ so
wishes, and so  I shall not mention the greetings and

expressions of respect with which you seek to flatter me nor the gentle words with which you strive to make your criticisms of me more acceptable; instead I shall pass straight to the points in question.

You say[6] that you received from one of the brothers a book of mine which bore no title but in which I gave a list of ecclesiastical writers both Greek and Latin; when you asked him - to use your own words - why the first page had no title on it and what its title was believed to be, he answered that it was called an obituary notice. Your reasoning is that it would be correctly so called if one were only to read in it of the lives and writings of people who were already dead, but since it mentions the works of many people who were alive at the time my book was written and are still alive, you think it strange that I should have given it this title. I would have thought that with your intelligence you would see that the title can be understood from the content of the work itself. You have read both Greek and Latin authors who have given accounts of the lives of distinguished men[7] - and you know they would never call these works of theirs 'An Obituary Notice', but 'The Deeds of Famous Men', in other words, accounts of the lives of leaders, philosophers, orators, historians, epic poets, and writers of tragedy and comedy, whereas an obituary is properly written for people who have died, like the one I recall I once wrote on the death of the presbyter Nepotianus of blessed memory.[8] And so this book should be called 'The Deeds of Famous Men', or more accurately, 'Ecclesiastical Writers', although a number of ignorant editors have entitled it 'Authors'.

Secondly you ask why, in my commentary on the epistle to the Galatians, I said that Paul could not have reprimanded Peter for something which Paul himself had done; in other words, he could not accuse someone else of pretence when he himself was guilty of it. You also assert that St. Paul's reprimand of Peter was not of a dispensatory nature but was genuine and that I ought not to teach that his words involved a lie but that everything written means what it says. In answer to this, my first point is that you ought to have remembered the short preface to my commentary[9] where I say, 'What then? Am I so stupid or rash as to promise something which Origen was unable to do? Certainly not. In fact I consider that I have been all the more cautious and wary in that, being aware of the weakness of my talents, I have followed Origen's commentary.[10] For he wrote five volumes of his own on the epistle of Paul to the Galatians and concluded the tenth book of his Stromateis [11] with a brief exposition of this commentary of his. He also composed various treatises and excerpts which could stand in their own right. I need not discuss the commentary of my friend Didymus with his prophetic sight, nor Apollinaris of Laodicea who recently left the Church, nor Alexander the old heretic, nor Eusebius of Emesa or Theodorus of Heraclea who have all left commentaries of their own on this subject.[12] If I were to select a few passages from these, they would be things which could not be utterly condemned. And I declare with absolute honesty that I have read them all and after mentally absorbing many things, I dictated my ideas - or the ideas of others - to my copyist, without keeping to the order or the words or even sometimes to the meanings. Now it is for the Lord of mercy to prevent things which have been well expressed by others from disappearing because of our ineptitude and things which are acceptable to one's own people from displeasing foreigners.

If then you considered anything in my explanation worthy of criticism, it was up to your learning to find out whether what I had written was to be found in the writings of the Greeks, so that if they had not said them, then you could justifiably condemn my opinion, especially since I openly confessed in my preface that I had followed the commentaries of Origen and had dictated either my own or other people's ideas. And at the end of the same chapter with which you find fault, I wrote,[13] 'If my meaning displeases anyone, it is for him to explain how it can be shown that Peter did not sin and that it was not insolent of Paul to accuse his superior; he must show what the consequences are of Paul criticising someone else for something which he himself committed.' I thereby made it clear that I was not defending unequivocally what I had read in the Greek authors but had expressed the ideas that I had read in such a way as to leave it to the reader to decide for himself whether to approve these things or not.[14]

Instead of doing what I had asked, you thought up a new argument, asserting that the Gentiles who had believed in Christ were free from the burden of the law, while those who were converts from Judaism were still subject to the law, so that in speaking for both groups of people Paul was right, as the teacher of the Gentiles, to criticise those who kept the law while Peter, as spokesman for those Christians who came over from the people of the circumcision, was justly criticised for commanding the Gentiles to do something which only those who had been Jews were supposed to observe. If, or rather because, this is the opinion you espouse, namely that all who have been converted from Judaism have a duty to keep the law,[15] you, as the most famous bishop in the whole world ought to spread this view and to induce all your fellow-bishops to agree with you; I, together with my monks, that is, my fellow sinners in this little hut of mine, do not dare to pronounce on such difficult matters but only venture to admit openly that I read the writings of my predecessors; and in my commentaries I give different explanations in accordance with common practice, so that each reader can follow whichever one of the many interpretations he prefers - I believe you, too, follow this method and approve of it both with regard to secular literature and Holy Scripture.

Origen was, however, the first to put forward the explanation I gave, in his exposition of the epistle of Paul to the Galatians in the tenth book of the Stromateis, and all later exegetes followed him. My reason for introducing it was primarily to answer Porphyry[16] who blasphemously accused Paul of having dared to reprimand Peter, the leading apostle, and censure him to his face, forcing Peter to admit that he had done wrong - in other words, Porphyry charged Paul with being guilty of the same error as Paul himself who accused Peter of acting wrongly. Should I mention John Chrysostom who a short time ago was bishop at Constantinople? He wrote a long book on the subject of this chapter in which he followed the views of Origen and other writers of old.[17] If, then, you criticise me for my error, allow me, I ask you, to err in the company of such men; when you perceive that I have many allies in my error, you will have to put forward at least one person who supports the truth of your opinion. All this on the question of the

interpretation of one chapter of the epistle to the
Galatians!

But as I do not wish to give you the impression
that my opposition to your view depends on the number
of my witnesses and that I am evading the truth,
relying on the support of distinguished men and not
daring to confront you, I shall briefly put forward
some pieces of evidence from Scripture. In the Acts of
the Apostles a voice says to Peter, 'Get up, Peter,
kill and eat (i.e. all fourfooted animals and reptiles
on the earth and all the birds of the sky.)' [Acts
10.13] These words show that no man is unclean by
nature but that all are equally called to the gospel of
Christ. Peter's reply to this was, 'No, for I have
never eaten anything common or unclean.' [Acts 10.14]
But then the voice spoke to him a second time saying,
'What God has purified, you must not call common.'
[Acts 10.15] And so he went to Caesarea and entering
Cornelius' house he opened his mouth and said, 'Truly I
perceive that God shows no partiality: anyone, from
whatever nation, who fears him and does what is right
is acceptable to him.' [Acts 10.34-35] And a few lines
later it says, 'The Holy Spirit fell on them and the
believers among the circumcised, who had come with
Peter, were amazed because the gift of the Holy Spirit
had been poured out even on the Gentiles. Then Peter
answered, 'Can anyone refuse water for baptizing these
who have received the Holy Spirit just like us?' And
he ordered that they should be baptised in the name of
Jesus Christ [Acts 10.44-48]. The apostles and the
brothers who were in Judea heard that the Gentiles had
also received the word of God. And when Peter had gone
up to Jerusalem, those who were circumcised criticised
him saying, 'Why did you go in to uncircumcised men and

eat with them?' [Acts 11.1-3] When Peter had given them a full explanation, he concluded his speech with these words, 'If then God gave the same gift to them as he gave to us who believed in the Lord Jesus Christ, who was I to withstand God?' When they heard this, they fell silent and glorified God, saying, 'Then to the Gentiles also God has granted repentance unto life.' [Acts 11.17-18]

And then, much later, when Paul and Barnabas reached Antioch and told the whole congregation there what God had done with them and that he had opened a door of faith to the Gentiles, some men came down from Judea and were teaching the brethren, saying, 'Unless you are circumcised according to the custom of Moses, you cannot be saved.' When a violent argument arose between them and Paul and Barnabas, they decided that both the accused and their accusers should go up to Jerusalem to see the apostles and elders about this problem [Acts 14.27-15.2]. On their arrival at Jerusalem some believers belonging to the party of the Pharisees rose up, saying, 'It is necessary to circumcise them and order them to keep the law of Moses,' [Acts 15.5] and there was a great debate about this statement; Peter then said with his usual frankness, 'Brothers, you know that from the early days God made choice among us that by my mouth the Gentiles should hear the word of the gospel and believe. And God who knows the heart bore witness to them, giving them the Holy Spirit just as he did to us; and he made no distinctions between us and them, cleansing their hearts by faith. Why then do you now urge God to put a yoke upon the neck of the disciples, which neither our fathers nor we have been able to bear? But we believe that we are saved by the grace of our Lord Jesus

Christ, just as they are.' [Acts 15.7-11] Then the whole crowd was silent and the apostle James and all the elders changed their minds in line with Peter's view.

The reader ought not to find these quotations tedious; he should find them just as useful as I do in demonstrating that even before the apostle Paul, Peter was not unaware of the decision of which he was in fact the author, to the effect that the law is not to be kept after the coming of Christ. Indeed, Peter had such great authority that Paul wrote in one of his letters, 'Then after three years I went to Jerusalem to visit Peter and I stayed with him for a fortnight,' [Gal. 1.18] and further on, 'After fourteen years I went up to Jerusalem again, taking Barnabas and Titus. I went up in accordance with a revelation and I laid before them the gospel which I preach among the Gentiles,' [Gal. 2.1-2] showing that he was not confident in his preaching of the gospel without the confirmation of Peter's opinion and that of the others with him. He goes on immediately afterwards, 'But privately before those who were of repute, lest somehow I should be running or had run in vain.' [Gal. 2.2] Why in private and not in public? To prevent it proving a stumbling block to the faith of those believers who had been converted from Judaism and who believed that the law must be kept and that this was a precondition for faith in the Lord and Saviour. And so, also at the time when Peter came to Antioch (although this is not recorded in the Acts of the Apostles, Paul confirms that it is true), Paul wrote that he opposed him to his face, 'because he was reprehensible.' [Gal. 2.11] Before certain men came from James, Peter ate with the Gentiles; but after they had come, he withdrew and set himself apart, fearing those Christians converted from Judaism. All the other Jews acted in the same way, so that even Barnabas was persuaded to imitate their pretence. 'But when I saw,' he writes, 'that they were not acting rightly and in accordance with the truth of the gospel, I said to Peter in the presence of all, "If you live as a Gentile and not as a Jew although you are a Jew, how can you force the Gentiles to live like Jews?" [Gal. 2.14] etc. Peter the apostle was undoubtedly initially responsible for this principle which he is now accused of violating. The reason for this violation was merely fear of the Jews, for Scripture says that he first ate with the Gentiles, but when certain people came from James, he withdrew and set himself apart for fear of the converts from Judaism. He feared that the Jews, whose apostle he was, might abandon their faith in Christ, using the Gentiles as a pretext and that he who had taken over from the Good Shepherd might lose the flock entrusted to him.[18]

And so, as I have shown, Peter did indeed have the right idea about abolishing the law of Moses but he was driven by fear to pretend to observe it; let us now consider whether Paul himself, who accused Peter, had acted in a similar way. In the Acts of the Apostles we also read that Paul went through Syria and Cilicia, strengthening the churches. He then came to Derbe and Lystra where there was a disciple called Timothy, whose mother was a Christian convert from Judaism while his father was Greek. He was well spoken of by the brothers at Lystra and Iconium and Paul wanted him to accompany him; he took Timothy and had him circumcised because of the Jews who were in that area, for they all knew that his father was Greek.[19] O blessed apostle

Paul, you who rebuke Peter for his hypocrisy in withdrawing from the Gentiles out of fear of the Jews who had come with James, why did you force Timothy to be circumcised contrary to your own belief, although he was the son of a Gentile and undoubtedly a Gentile himself? You will reply, 'On account of the Jews who were in that area.' If you can make excuses for yourself for having had a Gentile disciple circumcised, then you should also forgive Peter, your superior, for occasionally acting out of fear of those believers who had been Jews.

Elsewhere it is written that Paul, after staying many days (at Corinth), said goodbye to the brothers and sailed for Syria together with Priscilla and Aquila and that at Cenchreae he cut his hair because he had made a vow.[20]  It may be that Paul was forced to do what he did not want to, out of fear of the Jews; but why did he grow his hair because of a vow and later cut it at Cenchreae in accordance with the law? - something which the Nazarites who had devoted themselves to God used to do in accordance with the rules laid down by Moses.[21]

But these things are unimportant in comparison with what follows. Luke, who wrote an account of these sacred events, relates that when he and his companions came to Jerusalem, the brothers welcomed them gladly, and on the following day James and all the elders who were with Paul expressed their approval of his message and said to him, 'You see, brother, how many thousands there are in Judea who have believed in Christ, and all these are zealous for the law. But they have been told that you teach all the Jews who are among the Gentiles to forsake Moses, telling them not to circumcise their children or observe the Jewish customs. What then is to be done? We must at least call a meeting of all the people, for they will hear that you have come. Do therefore what we tell you. We have four men who are under a vow; take these men and purify yourself along with them and pay their expenses, so that they may shave their heads. Then all will know that there is nothing in what they have been told about you, but that you yourself live according to the law.' [Acts 21.17-24] So Paul took the men and the next day he purified himself with them and went into the temple to give notice when the days of purification would be fulfilled and the offering presented for every one of them. [Acts 21.26]

Paul, I must ask you again, why did you shave your head, why did you take part in the procession barefoot in accordance with the Jewish custom? Why did you offer sacrifices and allow victims to be slaughtered on your behalf in accordance with the law? No doubt you will answer that you did so to prevent the believers who had been Jews from being put off. So you pretended to be a Jew in order to bring the Jews over to your side, (22) having learnt this kind of hypocrisy from James and the other elders. But you still could not escape; an uprising occurred in which you were to be put to death, but you were snatched away by the tribune and sent to Caesarea under the watchful eye of a military guard, to prevent the Jews killing you as a hypocrite and destroyer of the law and then when you reached Rome, you preached Christ to both Jews and Gentiles in your lodgings and your beliefs were finally confirmed by Nero's sword. (23)

We have seen that both Peter and Paul pretended that they kept the precepts of the law for fear of the Jews. What cheek, what audacity for Paul to reprimand

someone else for something which he himself had done!
Not only I, but also others before me have given an
explanation of the case based on their own views, not
with the intention of defending a white lie, as you
allege, but of showing that it was a matter of honest
diplomacy; they wanted both to display the wisdom of
the apostles and to put a stop to Porphyry's blasphemy
and impudence.  For he alleged that Paul and Peter had
fought like children, or rather that Paul, in his envy
of Peter's virtues, had flared up and had
ostentatiously written an account of things which Peter
had not done or, if he had, then it was wrong of Paul
to rebuke Peter for something of which Paul himself was
guilty.

These exegetes interpreted this passage as best
they could.  As for you, how would you explain it?
Since you have criticised the view of earlier writers,
you will no doubt give a better explanation yourself.
In your letter you wrote to me,[(24)] 'For I should not
be the one to teach you how to understand that passage
where Paul says, "To the Jews I became as a Jew that I
might gain the Jews," [1 Cor. 9.20] and everything else
which he said out of mercy and compassion not through
deceit and pretence.  For a person who nurses a sick
man becomes like a sick person not by pretending to
have a fever but by thinking sympathetically how he
would like to be looked after if he himself were sick.
For Paul was without doubt a Jew and when he became a
Christian, he had not given up the practices of the
Jews which that people had accepted as being lawful and
suitable for the time.  He therefore undertook to
perform these things although he was already an apostle
of Christ, but he did so in order to show that they
were not harmful to those who wished to observe them as

they had received them from their parents by way of the law even after they had come to believe in Christ.  He wanted to show that Christians ought not to set their hope of salvation in these things, because the salvation which was signified by those sacraments had already come through the Lord Jesus.'

The point of your whole letter - which was considerably extended by your lengthy discussion - was that Peter's mistake did not lie in thinking that Christians who had been converted from Judaism must observe the law but in deviating from the path of truth by forcing the Gentiles to behave like Jews; and he forced them not by the authority of his teaching but by the example of his way of life.  You believe that Paul would not oppose something which he himself had done; the reason for his opposition was that Peter compelled those who had been Gentiles to behave like Jews.

The upshot, then, of your question, or rather of your statement, is that after the gospel of Christ the Jewish believers were right to keep the commandments of the law, in other words, to offer sacrifices as Paul did, to circumcise their sons as Paul did with Timothy, and to observe the sabbath, as all the Jews did.  If this is true, we are slipping into the heresies of Cerinthus and of the Ebionites[25] who have been condemned by the Fathers although they believe in Christ, for the sole reason that they combine the gospel of Christ with the rituals of the law, thereby professing their new faith without renouncing the old. What shall I say of the Ebionites who pretend to be Christians?  Down to this day, throughout all the synagogues of the East, that heresy (known as the Minaean)[26] persists among the Jews and is utterly condemned by the Pharisees who are commonly called

Nazarenes: they believe in Christ, the Son of God, born of the Virgin Mary and say that he suffered under Pontius Pilate and came back to life, just as we believe, but in wishing to be both Jews and Christians, they are neither Jews nor Christians. And so I beg you that instead of being concerned to heal my little wound - a mere pinprick if I may say so - you should heal the wound of this belief, inflicted by a spear or, if I may say so, a powerful catapult. To put forward the various views of earlier writers in one's explanation of Scripture is a very different fault from reintroducing a wicked heresy into the Church. But if it is incumbent upon us to welcome the Jews together with their legalistic customs, and if they are allowed to observe in the churches of Christ what they practised in the synagogues of Satan[27] - I speak my mind - then they will not become Christians but will make us Jews!

What Christian could listen without indignation to the following statement contained in your letter?[28] 'Paul was a Jew and when he became a Christian, he had not given up the practices of the Jews which that people had accepted as being lawful and suitable for the time. He therefore undertook to perform these things although he was already an apostle of Christ, but he did so in order to show that they were not harmful to those who wished to observe them as they had received them from their parents.' I beseech you once again: please do not be offended if I express my grief. Paul used to observe the Jewish rituals when he was already Christ's apostle, and you say that these were not dangerous for those who wished to observe them in the way they had received them from their parents; that is the opposite of what I say and I shall join in

the universal protests and openly declare that the
Jewish rituals are not only dangerous but deadly to
Christians and that anyone who observes them, whether
Jew or Gentile, will be cast down into hell.  For the
end of the law is Christ who brings righteousness to
all who have faith,[29] whether Jew or Gentile, but he
would not be the end bringing righteousness to all if
the Jew were excepted.  In the Gospel we read, 'The law
and the prophets down to John the Baptist' [Luke 16.16]
and in another passage, 'This was why the Jews sought
all the more to kill him because he not only failed to
observe the sabbath but also called God his father,
making himself equal with God,' [John 5.18] and in
another one, 'From his fullness have we all received
grace upon grace, because the law was given through
Moses, while grace and truth came through Jesus
Christ.' [John 1.16-17]  Instead of the grace of the
law, which came first, we have received the grace of
the gospel which is everlasting, and instead of the
shadows and types of the Old Testament, truth has come
through Jesus Christ.  Jeremiah also prophesied in the
name of God when he said, 'Behold the days are coming,
says the Lord, when I will fulfil for the house of
Israel and the house of Judah a new testament, not like
the testament which I gave to their fathers on the day
when I took their hand to lead them out of the land of
Egypt.' [Jerem. 31.31]  Notice what he says:  he
promises the new testament of the gospel not to the
Gentile nations with whom he had not previously made a
testament, but to the Jewish people, to whom he had
granted the law through Moses so that they would not
live according to the old letter, but in the newness of
the spirit.[30]  Paul, who is the subject of this
discussion, frequently expressed similar opinions, of

which I will quote but a few in the interests of brevity. 'Now I, Paul, say to you that if you are circumcised, Christ does not benefit you,' [Gal. 5.2] and, 'You have been severed from Christ, you who would be justified by the law; you have fallen away from grace,' [Gal. 5.4] and further on, 'If you are led by the Spirit, you are not now subject to the law.' [Gal. 5.18] From these statements it is clear that he who is subject to the law not, as our predecessors said, by way of accommodation to the divine purpose, but truly, as you believe, does not possess the Holy Spirit. God himself has informed us of the nature of the precepts of the law: 'I have given them precepts,' he says, 'which are not beneficial and ordinances by which they cannot live.' [Ezech. 20.25] We say this not in order to deny the importance of the law as the Manichees and Marcion[31] did, for we know that it is, in the words of the apostle, holy and spiritual,[32] but because with the coming of faith and the fullness of time, God sent his son, born of woman, born under the law, to redeem those who were under the law [Gal. 4.4-5] so that we might receive adoption as sons and live, not under the guidance of a guardian, but of an adult, our Lord and heir.[33]

In your letter you go on, 'And so he did not correct Peter for observing traditions which had been handed down to him by his fathers, because if Peter had wished to do so, he could have done so without deceit and would have been doing nothing wrong.' I repeat, you are a bishop, the teacher of the churches of Christ: if you want to prove the truth of what you assert, imagine a Jew who, after becoming a Christian, has his son circumcised, who observes the sabbath and abstains from foods which God created for use with

thanksgiving,[34] who on the fourteenth day of the
first month slaughters a lamb at evening; when you
have done this - but you will not do it for I know you
are a Christian and will not do anything sacrilegious -
you will reject your own opinion, whether you like it
or not and then you will learn that it is more
difficult to prove one's own argument than to criticise
another's.

But for fear that you might perhaps not have
persuaded us to believe or rather, for fear that we
might not understand what you were saying (for it often
happens that a protracted discussion is
incomprehensible, and because the ignorant do not
understand it, they are less likely to criticise it),
you emphasise your meaning by repeating, 'And so Paul
only abandoned the Jewish customs which were evil.'
What were the evil practices of the Jews rejected by
Paul? 'Failing to recognise God's righteousness and
wishing to establish their own form of righteousness,
they did not submit to the righteousness of God;[35]
and secondly the fact that after the passion and
resurrection of Christ, when the sacrament of grace had
been granted and revealed according to the order of
Melchisedech,[36] they still thought the old practices
should be celebrated, not out of respect for the
traditional ritual but because they were regarded as
necessary for salvation. However, if they had never
been necessary, then the martyrdom of the Maccabees[37]
in their defence would have been pointless and futile.
Finally Paul rejected the practice whereby the Jews
persecuted the Christian preachers of grace as if they
were enemies of the law. It is these misapprehensions
and faults and others like them which he says he
counted as loss and dung that he might gain

Christ.'(38)

You have informed us what evil practices of the
Jews Paul rejected. Let us learn from you also which
of their good practices he kept up. You say,(39) 'The
practices of the law which they celebrated in
accordance with the traditions of their fathers, just
as they had been celebrated by Paul himself, without
being necessary for salvation.' I do not quite
understand what you mean when you say, 'Without being
necessary for salvation.' If they do not bring
salvation, why do the Jewish Christians keep up these
practices? But if they have to be observed, they must
bring salvation, especially those practices whose
observation has produced martyrs, for they would not be
observed unless they brought salvation. On the other
hand they are not neutral, halfway between good and
bad,(40) as the philosophers argue. Continence is
good, self-indulgence is bad, while walking, for
example, would be a neutral act, neither good nor bad,
as would evacuating the bowels or blowing one's nose or
spitting out catarrh.(41) Such things are neither good
nor bad; whether you do them or not will not affect
your moral status, but to observe the rituals of the
law cannot be neither good nor bad - it must be either
one or the other. You say that it is good, I assert
that it is bad; bad not only for those of Gentile
origin but also for Jews who have been converted to
Christianity. On this question, unless I am mistaken,
you avoid one problem only to find yourself confronting
another, for in your fear of Porphyry's blasphemies,
you fall into the trap of the Ebionites when you say
that converts from Judaism must observe the law. And
because you recognise that what you say has dangerous
implications, you then try to tone it down by

unnecessarily adding these words, 'Without any belief
that they were necessary for salvation, as the Jews
believed or that they must be kept as a deceitful
pretence, which is what Paul had rebuked Peter for.'
And so Peter was only pretending to observe the law but
Paul, who rebuked him, practised without fear rituals
which were legitimate. For you go on in your letter,
'If he took part in these rituals by pretending to be a
Jew in order to win them over, why did he not also
sacrifice with the Gentiles, putting himself outside
the law as they were outside the law, so that he might
win them too? Was it not because he practised the
Jewish rituals as one who was by nature a Jew and said
all this not in order to pretend deceitfully to be what
he was not, but feeling he ought to help them
compassionately, as if he himself were liable to the
same error; and so he was not acting with the cunning
of a liar but with the love of one who feels
compassion.' You are right to defend Paul: but
according to you he did not pretend to accept the error
of the Jews - he really did share their error. He did
not wish to imitate Peter's dishonesty in covering up
what he was for fear of the Jews - instead he admitted
quite frankly to being a Jew. A strange example of
compassion on the part of the apostle! While wishing
to make the Jews Christians, he himself became a Jew!
We must conclude that he would have been unable to
bring the self-indulgent back to a life free from
excess unless he had proved himself to be self-
indulgent, nor could he have shown mercy to the
wretched unless he himself experienced wretchedness, as
you put it. Wretched indeed and worthy of pity are
they whose own contentiousness and devotion to the law
which has been abolished have led them to make the

apostle of Christ a Jew.

In fact there is not much difference between your
opinion and mine: I say that both Peter and Paul,
through fear of the Jewish-Christians, practised, or
rather pretended to practise, the prescriptions of the
law, while you maintain that they did this out of
compassion, not with an intention to deceive. That is
all right as long as it is agreed that, whether
motivated by fear or kindness, they pretended to be
what they were not. But the other argument which you
use against me, namely that if Paul became a Jew for
the Jews, he ought to have become a Gentile for the
Gentiles, supports my view more than yours. For just
as he was not truly a Jew, neither was he truly a
Gentile, and just as he was not truly a Gentile,
neither was he truly a Jew. He only imitated the
Gentiles in so far as he allowed Christians to avoid
circumcision and to eat foods indiscriminately - foods
which the Jews condemned - not, as you propose, because
he worshipped idols; for in Christ Jesus neither
circumcision nor uncircumcision has any importance,[42]
but only the keeping of God's commandments.

I therefore ask you and entreat you again and again
to pardon my little dispute. If I have overstepped the
limits you should admit that it is your fault, seeing
that it was you who forced me to write a reply and who
robbed me of my sight, as happened to Stesichorus.
Please do not think that I am advocating lies, for I
follow Christ who said, 'I am the way, the truth and
the life' [John 14.6] and it is impossible for me,
devoted to truth as I am, to submit to the yoke of
deceit. Nor must you incite the ignorant rabble
against me, those who respect you as their bishop and
who welcome you with the honour due to a priest when

you preach in the church. For me, however, in my
extreme old age, virtually decrepit as I am and living
in rural seclusion in my monastery, they have little
respect. Find yourself some other people to teach and
criticise because such vast distances across land and
sea separate me from you that the sound of your voice
hardly reaches me. If you do occasionally write me a
letter make sure it is delivered to me, to whom it is
addressed, before they receive it in Italy and Rome.

As to the question in your other letter[43] of why
my earlier translations of the canonical writings had
asterisks and commas marked, while my later translation
omitted such critical signs - with all respect I must
say that you do not appear to understand what you ask.
For the former translation is from the Septuagint and
wherever there are commas, like little daggers, it
indicates that the Septuagint expands on the Hebrew
text, while where there are asterisks, like little
stars shining onto the following words, something has
been added by Origen from the edition of Theodotion.
The first translation was made from the Greek, while
the second I made direct from the Hebrew and it
translates the true meaning, as I understood it,
without necessarily preserving the word order.[44] I
am surprised that you are not reading the Septuagint in
the original form as it was produced by the Seventy,
but in an edition corrected, or corrupted, by Origen
using daggers and asterisks and that you are not
following the translation, undistinguished though it
may be, of a Christian, especially when he has removed
those additions which came from the edition of a
Jew[45] and blasphemer after Christ's passion. Do you
wish to be a true admirer of the Septuagint? Then you
should not read what is preceded by an asterisk - in

fact you should delete such passages from your copy, to prove yourself to be a supporter of the ancient translators. But if you were to do this, you would be forced to condemn all church libraries for only one or two copies are to be found which do not contain these passages.

Then you say that I ought not to have followed the ancient texts in my translation but you use a strange syllogism to prove this! You write,[46] 'What was translated by the Seventy was either obscure or obvious. If it was obscure, it must be possible for you also to have been mistaken, while if it was obvious, it is clear that the Seventy could not have been mistaken.' I shall answer this objection using your own argument. All the earlier exegetes who preceded us in the Lord and who wrote commentaries on the Holy Scriptures gave explanations either of obscure passages or ones whose meaning was obvious. If they were obscure, how do you dare, after their attempts, to explain something which they were unable to explain? If obvious, it is unnecessary for you to try to explain what was clear to them, especially in your interpretation of the psalms for which there exist many volumes of commentaries by Greek writers such as Origen, Eusebius of Caesarea, Theodore of Heraclea, Asterius of Scythopolis, Apollinaris of Laodicea and Didymus of Alexandria.[47] There are also said to be short works on a few psalms by various writers, but now I am talking about commentaries on the whole corpus of the psalms. Among Latin writers there are Hilary of Poitiers and Eusebius of Vercellae who produced Latin versions of the commentaries of Origen and Eusebius, while even our friend Ambrose followed the former on some points.[48] Please tell me why your opinion should differ from that of such distinguished commentators on the psalms. If the psalms are unintelligible you must admit that it is possible for you, too, to be mistaken about them, but if their meaning is clear, it is hardly likely that those commentators should have got them wrong. And so, either way your interpretation will be redundant. On this principle no one will dare to express their view once their predecessors have spoken and whatever ground one person has covered will be out of bounds to any later writers. No, it should rather be your duty, as a civilised human being, to show the same indulgence to others as to yourself. I have not attempted to do away with the works of my predecessors which I emended and translated from Greek into Latin for those who spoke my language, but rather to publish the evidence which had been overlooked or corrupted by the Jews, so that Latin-speakers might know what was really in the Hebrew text. If someone does not wish to read my version, he will not be forced to do so against his will. Let him drink the old wine with enjoyment and reject my unfermented wine which was offered as an explanation of the commentaries of earlier writers with the intention of clarifying what was unintelligible.

As to the question of what method one should follow in interpreting the Holy Scriptures, this is dealt with in the book which I wrote entitled, 'The Best Method of Translation',[49] as well as in all the short prefaces which I wrote for each divine book and added to my edition; I think that the serious reader should be referred to these. And if, as you say, you approve of my revision of the New Testament, the reason you give for your approval being that there are many people with a knowledge of Greek who can judge my work,

then you ought to believe that my work on the Old
Testament is equally authentic, for in it I did not
include my own ideas but only translated the divine
texts as I found them in the Hebrew.  If you do not
believe me, ask the Hebrew scholars.  You may perhaps
say, 'What if the Hebrew scholars refuse to answer or
wilfully give a wrong answer?'  Will the whole Jewish
population keep silent about my translation?  Will it
be impossible to find anyone who has a knowledge of
Hebrew or will they all follow the example of those
Jews in some small African town who, according to you,
have conspired to misrepresent me?  For this is the
tale you tell in your letter:[50] 'When one of our
fellow bishops arranged for your translation to be read
in the church in his diocese, they came across a word
in your version of the prophet Jonah which you had
rendered very differently from the translation with
which they were familiar and which, having been read by
so many generations, was ingrained in their memories.
A great uproar ensued in the congregation, especially
among the Greeks who criticised the text and
passionately denounced it as wrong, and the bishop (the
incident took place in the city of Oea) was forced to
ask the Jews to give evidence.  Whether out of
ignorance or spite, they replied that this word did
occur in the Hebrew manuscripts in exactly the same
form as in the Greek and Latin versions.  In short, the
man was forced to correct the passage in your version
as if it were inaccurate since he did not want to be
left without a congregation as a result of this crisis.
This makes even us suspect that you, too, can be
mistaken occasionally.'  You allege that I made a
mistake in my translation of the prophet Jonah and that
the bishop almost lost his congregation when the people

rioted in protest because of a difference of one word. You fail to mention what it was that I mistranslated, thereby depriving me of a chance to defend myself; maybe you were afraid that my answer might make it clear that there were no grounds for an objection. Perhaps you are referring to the fact that many years ago, 'gourd' cropped up, when Cornelius and Asinius Pollio insisted that I had translated 'ivy' for 'gourd'. I have discussed this problem at greater length in my commentary on the prophet Jonah;[51] now it is enough for me just to say that in the passage where the Septuagint gives 'gourd' and Aquila and the rest translate 'ivy' i.e. kitton, the Hebrew text has 'ciceion' which the Syriac speakers commonly call 'ciceia.' There is a kind of shrub with broad leaves like a pumpkin; when it is planted it grows quickly into a bush without the support of any of the poles or props which cucumbers and ivy need, supporting itself on its own stem. If I had wanted to give a literal translation and used the word 'ciceion,' no one would have understood it; if I had translated it as 'gourd' I would be putting something which was not in the Hebrew, so I put 'ivy' to be in agreement with other translators. But if your Jews, as you claim, whether out of spite or ignorance, said that the Hebrew edition contained the same as the Greek and Latin editions, it is clear that they are either ignorant of Hebrew literature or that they deliberately lied so as to make fun of the gourd planters.

Now at the end of my letter I ask you not to force an old man, once an experienced soldier but now discharged, to fight and once again to risk his life. You are a young man, firmly established at the summit of episcopal dignity: teach your people and fill the

Roman storerooms with the fruits of Africa. I am satisfied to whisper to one poor listener or reader in some little corner of my monastery.

NOTES

1. Augustine's Ep. 28, Ep. 40 and Ep. 71.

2. 1 Sam. 17.40-51.

3. 2 Chron. 26.19-20.

4. 2 Cor. 12.14.

5. 1 Chron. 12.17-18.

6. Aug. Ep. 40.2.

7. Suetonius' work De Viris Illustribus (only partially extant) was Jerome's most notable model, but in his preface [P.L. 23.603] Jerome mentions several authors, both Greek and Roman, who wrote similar works.

8. Jer. Ep.60 to Heliodorus on the death of Nepotian [CSEL 54.548-575].

9. Jerome's preface to his Commentary on the Epistle to the Galatians [P.L. 26.308f.].

10. Origen's commentary is mostly lost, existing now only in three fragments in Pamphilus' apology for Origen [P.G. 14.1293-8] and in excerpts in Jerome's work.

11. Origen's Stromateis survives only in a few fragments; in it Origen seems to have attempted to interpret Christian concepts using the language of Platonic philosophy, as well as dealing with Scriptural problems.

12. In his De Viris Illustribus [P.L. 23] Jerome includes all these Greek writers of commentaries on the epistle to the Galatians (except Alexander, who was

possibly the Valentinian heretic with whom Tertullian entered into a controversy over the Incarnation). Didymus was a fourth century head of the school at Alexandria, blind from childhood; Apollinaris (c. 310-390) was the heresiarch whose views involved a partial denial of Christ's true humanity; Eusebius was bishop of Emesa in Syria (for his commentary, see P.G. 86) while Theodorus was bishop of Heraclea in Thrace.

13. Jer. Comm. in Gal. 2.14 [P.L. 26.342].

14. Cf. Jer. Apol. cont. Ruf. I.15-29 [CCL 79.13-29].

15. Cf. Gal. 5.3.

16. Porphyry (232-305) the Neoplatonist was a forceful opponent of Christianity (see e.g. Chadwick p. 117); for his attack on Paul and Peter, see the preface to Jerome's commentary on Galatians [P.L. 26. 310-11].

17. John Chrysostom was bishop of Constantinople between 398 and 404 before he was driven into exile; the work referred to by Jerome is either Chrysostom's commentary on the epistle to Galatians [P.G. 61] or his homily 'In faciem ei restiti' [P.G. 51].

18. Cf. John 21.15-27.

19. Acts 15.41-16.3.

20. Acts 18.18.

21. Cf. Num. 6.18.

22. Cf. 1 Cor. 9.20.

23. Cf. Acts 23.12-24; 28.14,30. There is no record in the N.T. of Paul's death but Eusebius records that he died in the Neronian persecution.

24. Aug. Ep. 40.4.

25. Cerinthus was a Jewish Gnostic of the first century A.D.; Irenaeus (Adv. Haer. III.11.1) says that St. John wrote his Gospel in answer to Cerinthus. The Ebionites were a group of Jewish Christians in the first century who were regarded as outside the mainstream by both Jews and Christians.

26. The Minaei formed a Jewish heretical sect, while the Nazarenes were Jewish Christians who continued to

obey much of the Jewish law but were regarded as heretical by Jews.

27. For the term 'synagogues of Satan', see Rev. 2.9; 3.9.

28. Aug. Ep. 40.4.

29. Cf. Rom. 10.4.

30. Cf. Rom. 7.6.

31. The Manichaean heretics rejected the Old Testament, as had the heretical Marcion who accepted only a Gospel of Love which found no room for the stern Jewish God of the O.T. On the Manichees and the Old Testament and Augustine's early attraction to them, see Brown pp. 49-50,53.

32. Cf. Rom. 7.12,14.

33. Cf. Gal. 3.25; 4.1,7.

34. Cf. 1 Tim. 4.3.

35. Cf. Rom. 10.3.

36. Ps. 109.4 (110.4); Hebr. 5.6.

37. 2 Macc. 7.

38. Cf. Phil. 3.8.

39. Aug. Ep. 40.6.

40. Cf. Aug. Ep. 82.13. 'Indifferens' was a technical term in Stoic philosophy (cf. Cic. De Fin. III.16.53) applied to things regarded as morally neutral.

41. I here follow the text of Goldbacher [CSEL 34.311] in his edition of Augustine's Ep. 75, taking the words 'continence...catarrh' as Jerome's own words rather than as the reported speech of the philosophers, as Hilberg and Schmid do. It is surely quite characteristic of Jerome to mention bodily functions.

42. Cf. Gal. 5.6; 6.15.

43. Aug. Ep. 71.

44. Cf. Jer. Ep. 57.5 [CSEL 54.508] in a letter to Pammachius on the best method of translation where Jerome writes, 'I openly admit that where the order of the words was a mystery I did not translate word for word, but tried to express the true sense.'

45. i.e. Theodotion (ii A.D.), the Jewish translator of the O.T. from Hebrew into Greek; cf. Jer. De Vir. Illustr. 54 [P.L. 23.665] where Jerome refers to him as an Ebionite.

46. Aug. Ep. 28.2.

47. Only fragments of the commentaries on the psalms by the Greek writers to whom Jerome refers here are still extant, although Origen wrote a great deal on the psalms and the writings of Eusebius of Caesarea had a high reputation (cf. Jer. De Vir. Illustr. 81 [P.L. 23.689]; see P.G. 23 for the fragments of Eusebius). The fragments of Didymus' commentary are to be found in P.G. 39. It is unclear who Asterius of Scythopolis was.

48. In his commentaries on the psalms [P.L. 9] Hilary of Poitiers followed Origen closely, while Eusebius of Vercellae translated the commentary of Eusebius of Caesarea (the translation is now lost). Ambrose's commentaries on a small selection of psalms are to be found in P.L. 14 and 15.

49. i.e. Jer. Ep. 57 to Pammachius [CSEL 54.503-526].

50. See Aug. Ep. 71.5.

51. Jer. Comm. in Ionam 4.6 [CCL 76.1.414] for an earlier reference to Cornelius and Asinius Pollio; see also P. Antin in his edition of the commentary [p. 109 n. 1] for an explanation of these enigmatic references. On the question of the gourd and the ivy and Rufinus' criticism at Rome, see Rufinus' Apology against Jerome II.35 [P.L. 21.614].

JEROME EP. 115

To my truly holy lord and most blessed bishop Augustine, Jerome sends greetings in Christ.

Being anxious to learn from my holy brother[1] how you were, I was glad to hear that you were well. Then, as I was - I will not say hoping for, but rather demanding a letter from you, he told me that he had left Africa without your knowledge. I am therefore paying my respects to you through him, for he loves you with an unparallelled devotion, and I beg you to forgive my shame: you have begged me many times to reply and I could not refuse. But it was not I who answered you, but one argument answering another, and if I was at fault in answering (I ask you to listen without indignation), you were much more at fault for provoking me. But enough of these recriminations; let there exist between us pure brotherly love and let us send each other letters full of love instead of criticism.

The holy brothers who serve the Lord with us, send their warmest greetings. I beg you to send my regards to the holy brothers who bear the light yoke of Christ with you,[2] especially the holy and beloved Alypius. May Christ our omnipotent God keep you safe and mindful of me, my truly holy lord and most blessed bishop. If you have .read my commentary on Jonah, I think that you will not dwell on the ridiculous problem of the gourd. But if the friend[3] who first attacked me with the sword has been driven back by the pen, it is up to your goodness and justice to rebuke the accuser, not the defendant. Please let us sport on the field of

Scripture without hurting each other.

NOTES

1. The messenger may have been Firmus, a name which appears in one MS [R]; Goldbacher [CSEL 34.350] accepts this reading.  On Firmus cf. Aug. Ep. 82.1.

2. Cf. Matt. 11.30.

3. Jerome probably means Rufinus, his former friend.

AUGUSTINE EP. 82

It is now a long time since I sent you a lengthy letter[1] in reply to yours[2] - the one, you recall, which you gave for delivery to your holy son Asterius, who is now not only my brother but also my colleague. I do not yet know whether my letter reached you; I only know from what you write in the letter[3] delivered by our most reliable brother Firmus, that if he who was the first to attack you with the sword has been driven back by the pen, it is my duty to act with goodness and justice and rebuke the accuser, not the defendant. Slight as it is, this is the only indication I have which leads me to suppose that you have read that letter of mine. Yes, it is true; I did lament[4] the fact that such discord should have arisen between the two of you, whose intimate friendship, wherever its fame had spread, was a source of joy to all who loved you as brothers. In doing so I was not rebuking you - I would not venture to attribute any blame to you in this matter - but I was expressing my sadness at the misfortune of human existence, for however strong the love which unites men in friendship, it is uncertain how long it will continue. I would have preferred to know from your own reply whether you have forgiven me as I asked.[5] I would like you to give me a clearer assurance of this, although it is true that the cheerful tone of your letter appears to indicate that I have obtained your forgiveness - if of course it was sent after you had read mine,[6] something which your letter does not make clear.

You ask, or rather you command, confident of the

love between us, that we should sport on the field of
Scripture without hurting each other.(7) To be honest,
as far as I am concerned I would prefer to discuss
Scriptural problems in a serious manner, not for
amusement. But if you chose this phrase as a friendly
joke, I must admit that I expect something better from
the abundance of your talents, from your wisdom and
learning and from your hard work which has continued
unabated for many years with great assiduity and
ability; the Holy Spirit has not only granted you this
achievement but has actually dictated it to you, so
that on questions of great importance and difficulty
you might assist me, for I am not so much sporting on
the field of Scripture as panting up the mountainside!
But if you thought you had to say, 'Let us sport' to
indicate the good-humour which ought to exist in
discussions between good friends, whether the subject
of our discussion is something clear and easy or
whether it is complicated and difficult, please let me
know how we can achieve this; after all, it may happen
that we come across a passage which embarrasses us in
that we cannot approve of its sense, (if not because of
lack of attention, then due to our slow understanding),
so that we try to assert the opposite interpretation.
If we are rather forthright in expressing our view, we
should not be suspected of childish boastfulness as if
we were seeking fame for ourselves by criticising
distinguished men;(8) but if when we make some rather
sharp remark in order to refute the other's argument,
we try to temper it with milder language, we should not
be accused of drawing a sword coated with honey(9) -
unless perhaps the only way of avoiding both these
faults themselves and the suspicion of the faults in
carrying on a discussion with a more learned friend, is

to approve  whatever he says and not be allowed to contradict it at all, even for the sake of our inquiry. Then, of course, it would be possible to sport on a field without  fear of giving offence, but I wonder whether we are not deluding ourselves.

I confess to you that I have learned to respect and honour only those books of the Scriptures now referred to as canonical.[10]  I firmly believe that none of the authors of these books has erred in writing, and if I should find fault with anything in them which appears to conflict with the truth, I am sure that the reason must be that there is some textual error or that the translator did not follow what was said or that I do not  understand it properly.  When I read other authors, however holy and learned they may be, I do not think something is true just because they believed it but because they can persuade me either by referring to those canonical authors or in view of a reasonable probability that their opinion is not at odds with the truth.  I am sure, my brother, that you are of the same opinion; furthermore, I do not think that you want your books to be read as if they had been written by prophets or apostles,  whose writings we must believe are free from all error.  Such a thought would conflict with your attitude of pious humility and with your true opinion of yourself - if you did not have these qualities you would not have said, 'I wish that I might deserve to embrace you and to converse with you, so that each of us might learn and teach something.'[11]

But if a consideration of your life and character leads me to believe that you spoke without pretence or deceit, is it not much more reasonable that I should believe that there was no discrepancy between what the

apostle Paul thought and wrote when he said of Peter
and Barnabas, 'When I saw that they were not living as
they should live, in accordance with the true words of
the gospel, I said to Peter in the presence of all, "If
you live as a Gentile and not as a Jew although you are
a Jew, how can you force the Gentiles to live like
Jews?"'? [Gal. 2.14] How can I be certain that he is
not deceiving me either in what he writes or what he
says, if he was deceiving his sons to whom he was
giving  birth a second time until Christ, that is the
truth, should be formed in them?[12] When he sent them
forth he said to them, 'In the things which I write to
you, behold before God, I do not lie'. [Gal. 1.20] Was
he not then writing truthfully but deceiving them with
some kind of prudent dissimulation, when he said that
he had seen Peter and Barnabas not living as they
should live in accordance with the true words of the
gospel and that he had rebuked Peter to his face for no
other reason than that he was forcing the Gentiles to
live like Jews?

But surely, someone might say, it is better to
believe that the apostle Paul wrote something
untruthful than that he did something wrong? If this
is the case, we might say - though God forbid - that it
is better to believe that the Gospels are lying than
that Christ was denied by Peter[13] and better to
believe that the Book of Kings is lying than that such
a great prophet as David, chosen by the Lord God in
such a remarkable way, committed adultery by desiring
and seducing another man's wife and was guilty of a
gruesome murder in killing her husband.[14] On the
contrary, since the Holy Scriptures are founded on the
highest summit of divine authority, I will read them
convinced and assured of their truth; I would rather

learn from them that men were really approved or corrected or condemned than feel that the divine words have become suspect to me at every point because I occasionally hesitate to believe that certain excellent and praiseworthy people have committed reprehensible deeds.[15]

The Manichees claim that a large number of passages of Holy Scripture are false[16] because they are unable to twist them to give an alternative meaning, but their wicked error is refuted by the clear meaning of these passages. Their claim is made in such a way that they avoid attributing such falsehood to the writings of the apostles - in this case they blame certain corrupters of the texts. However, as they were unable ever to prove their claim either by producing more texts or older ones, or by the authority of an older language from which the Latin books were translated, they were defeated by a truth so obvious to everyone and withdrew perplexed. Do you not understand what a great opportunity we provide for their malice if we say not that the apostolic writings were falsified by others but that the apostles themselves wrote lies?

It is incredible, you say,[17] that Paul should have reprimanded Peter for something which he himself had done. I am not now inquiring what he did; I am asking what he wrote. This has considerable bearing on the problem I am tackling in the belief that the truth of Holy Scripture has been handed down to posterity to build up our faith, not by any chance writers but by the apostles themselves; having thus been granted the sanction of the highest canonical authority, it may continue in all respects true and undoubted. For if Peter acted properly, then Paul lied when he said he saw him not living as he should in accordance with the true words of the gospel. A person who does what he should is surely acting rightly, and so anyone who says that he was not acting rightly in doing what he knew he ought to do is telling a lie. But if Paul did write the truth, then it is true that Peter was not at that time living as he should in accordance with the true words of the gospel - in other words he was doing what he ought not to do. And if Paul himself had already done something similar, I would sooner believe that having himself been corrected, he could not refrain from correcting his fellow apostle, than that he had made a false accusation in one of his letters; this is true of any of his letters but especially of that one in which he had already written, 'In what I write to you, I call God to witness, I do not lie.' [Gal. 1.20]

For my part I believe that Peter did act with the intention of forcing the Gentiles to live like Jews, for I read that Paul wrote this and I do not believe that he lied.[18] Therefore Peter was not right to act in this way, for he was going against the truth of the gospel in making those who believed in Christ think that they could not be saved without these ancient customs. This was what the converts from Judaism at Antioch claimed, against whom Paul fought bitterly and persistently. But this was not the reason why Paul himself had Timothy circumcised or fulfilled his vow at Cenchreae or why, when advised by James at Jerusalem, he undertook the celebration of those legitimate rites together with those who were under a vow.[19] He did not do these things to make people believe that Christian salvation depended on these sacraments; no, he did so to prevent them thinking that those things which God had fittingly ordered to be performed in earlier times as a prefiguration of future things[20]

were to be condemned like the idolatrous practices of
the Gentiles. This is what James told him was rumoured
about him[21] - that he advocated separation from
Moses; but it is evidently wrong that those who believe
in Christ should separate themselves from Christ's
prophet as if they abominated and condemned his
teaching, when Christ himself said of him, 'If you
believe Moses, you should also believe me, for it was
about me that he wrote.' [John 5.46]

I ask you to consider James' actual words. 'You
see, brother,' he said, 'how many thousands there are
among the Jews who have believed in Christ and these
are all zealous for the law. For they have been told
that you teach those Jews who are among the Gentiles to
forsake Moses, telling them not to circumcise their
children or observe the customs. What then is to be
done? We must certainly assemble the crowd for they
will hear that you have come. So do what we tell you.
Here are four men who are under a vow. Take them and
purify yourself along with them and pay their expenses,
so that they may shave their heads. All will then know
that everything they have heard about you is false and
that you do indeed follow the law and keep it. But
concerning the Gentiles who have believed, we have
given them orders, in the conviction that they should
observe none of these rituals except that they should
abstain from what has been sacrificed to idols and from
blood and fornication.' [Acts 21.20-25]

It is clear, in my opinion, that James gave this
advice so that those Jews who had continued to be
zealous for the law after coming to believe in Christ
should know that what they had been told about Paul was
false, namely that the commandments prescribed by God
and granted to their fathers by Moses should be

regarded as condemned as sacrilegious by the teaching of Christ. This rumour about Paul had not been spread by those who understood the spirit in which it was proper for these things to be observed at that time by the Jewish converts (in other words, so as to honour the divine authority and the prophetic holiness of the sacraments rather than so as to obtain salvation, which was now revealed in Christ and granted through the sacrament of baptism); no, those who spread this rumour about him were those who claimed that these customs must be observed, as if without them there could be no salvation in the Gospel for believers. These people realised that he was a very powerful preacher of grace and strongly opposed to their beliefs, in that he taught that man is not justified by these rituals but by the grace of Jesus Christ; the observance of these rituals, prefiguring the coming of Christ, had been obligatory under the law. Plotting to rouse hatred and persecution against him, they accused him of being an enemy of the law and the divine commandments and the only way Paul was able to avoid the hatred awakened by their false accusation was by himself performing these rites, which he was thought to condemn as sacrilegious. He thereby showed that the Jews were not forbidden to observe them as being wicked at that period but neither were the Gentiles forced to observe them as if they were necessary. [22]

If he had in fact been rejecting these rites as was said of him, but agreed to perform them so that he could conceal his true views through an act of pretence, James would not have said to him, 'And all will know' [Acts 21.24] but rather, 'And all will think' that what they had heard about him was false, especially since, although the apostles had already

decided in Jerusalem itself that no one should force
the Gentiles to live like Jews,[23] they had not
decided that it was necessary to forbid the Jews at
that period to live like Jews even though the Christian
teaching no longer compelled them to do so. Therefore,
if after the apostles' decision, Peter acted
deceitfully in that way at Antioch in forcing the
Gentiles to live like Jews (even though he himself was
not forced to do so, although because of the message of
God entrusted to the Jews[24] he was not forbidden to
do so), is it surprising if Paul constrained him to
declare openly the decision Peter remembered he had
made at Jerusalem with the other apostles?

But if, as I think is more likely, Peter did this
before that meeting at Jerusalem,[25] it is even so not
surprising that Paul wanted him to assert confidently
what he already knew they both agreed on, instead of
concealing it out of timidity; Paul wanted this either
because he had discussed the gospel with Peter or
because at the time of the calling of the centurion
Cornelius Paul realised that Peter had received a
warning from God about this or because before the
arrival at Antioch of those whom he feared he had seen
Peter eating with the Gentiles. I am not denying that
Peter was already at this stage in agreement with Paul,
so there was no need for Paul to tell him what the
truth was on this subject; he was only reprimanding his
hypocrisy in forcing the Gentiles to live like Jews.
He had no other reason for doing this except that all
such pretences were undertaken as if there was truth in
what was said by those who thought that believers could
not be saved without circumcision and the other
observances which were figures of things to come.[26]
That was also why he had Timothy circumcised[27] - in

case the Jews, especially those among his mother's
relations, should think that Gentile converts to Christ
rejected circumcision in the same way as idolatry had
to be condemned; whereas, in fact, God had commanded
men to practise circumcision, while it was Satan who
persuaded men to idolatry. On the other hand, Paul did
not have Titus circumcised for he did not want to
provide an opportunity to those who said that believers
could not be saved without circumcision or allow them
to assert, in their desire to deceive the Gentiles,
that Paul also believed this. Paul himself made this
abundantly clear when he said, 'But even though Titus
who was with me was a Greek, he was not compelled to be
circumcised, although that course was urged on account
of certain false brethren secretly brought in, who
infiltrated to spy on our freedom with the aim of
bringing us into bondage; but we did not yield to them
even for a moment, wishing as we did to ensure the
preservation of the gospel for you.' [Gal. 2.3-5] Here
it is clear that he had understood their intentions and
so he did not do what he had done in the case of
Timothy because he felt free to show that those
sacraments should neither be required as necessary nor
condemned as sacrilegious.[28]

We must of course be careful in this
discussion[29] for in trying to avoid saying, as the
philosophers do, that some human actions are neutral,
half-way between right and wrong and to be classified
neither as right actions nor as sins, we might be
forced (because it is impossible for the observance of
the rituals of the law to be neutral and because it
must be either good or bad), if we call it good, to
observe the rituals ourselves, while if we say such
observance is bad, we might have to believe that the

apostles had practised them disingenuously rather than sincerely. In fact, it is not so much the example of the philosophers that I fear for the apostles, for they do express some truths in their discussions; it is rather that of the forensic lawyers that I fear when they lie in defending other men's cases.[30] If it is regarded as proper to use such men as a comparison in an account of the epistle to the Galatians in order to prove the hypocrisy of Peter and Paul, why should I fear to mention the philosophers to you? They are not untrustworthy because everything they say is wrong but because most of the things they put their trust in are wrong and even when they happen to be saying true things, they are far from the grace of Christ who is truth itself.[31]

Why then should I not say that the orders given regarding the ancient sacraments are neither good (because men are not justified by them, for they are just figures foretelling the grace by which we are justified)[32] nor bad (because they were prescribed by God as suitable for the time and people)? My view is supported also by the prophet's statement in which God says he has given that people statutes which were not good.[33] Perhaps he did not mean that they were bad but only that they were not good; in other words, they were incapable of making men good but their absence did not prevent men becoming good. I would like you to tell me whether a Christian from the East who comes to Rome would be hypocritical if he fasted on the sabbath, except on the day of the Easter vigil. If we were to say this was wrong, we would be condemning not only the Roman church but also many neighbouring churches and some rather further away where this custom persists; but if we consider it wrong not to fast on the sabbath,

we will rashly be incriminating many Eastern churches
and by far the greater part of the Christian world! Do
you agree that we should say that it lies somewhere
between the two, being acceptable to someone who does
it not as a pretence but in order to observe the proper
customs of his society? And yet we do not read in the
canonical books that the Christians were ordered to do
any such thing. This makes me less willing to call an
evil what I cannot deny, even from the standpoint of
the Christian faith, that God prescribed, although this
faith teaches me that I am not justified by practising
this but only by the grace of God through our Lord
Jesus Christ.

I therefore declare that circumcision and other
such things were given by God to an earlier people by
means of the so-called Old Testament, to act as a sign
of future events which were to be fulfilled by Christ.
When these events came to pass, these observances
remained to be read about by Christians to enable them
to understand the prophecy which had been sent in
advance; there was no necessity to observe them as if
they were still waiting for the revelation of faith -
the future coming of which was indicated by these
rites. But even though these rituals were not to be
imposed on the Gentiles, they did not have to be
removed from the Jewish customs as if they had to be
detested and condemned. Slowly and gradually the
preaching of Christ's grace spread and believers
came to understand that by means of it alone would
they be justified and saved, not by those shadows of
events, formerly in the future but now present and at
hand; as a result, in calling the Jews who were found
living in this way at the time of Christ's physical
presence and during the apostolic period, all that

activity of shadows would disappear. Sufficient approval of these rites was shown by the fact that they were not to be rejected as detestable and idolatrous, but they would develop no further in case they should be considered necessary, as if salvation were dependent on them or impossible without them; this was what those heretics believed who wished to be both Jews and Christians but ended up by being neither Jewish nor Christian. You very kindly warned me[34] to beware of their belief, though I have never held it. Fear caused Peter to pretend that he held this belief, not to agree with it, so what Paul wrote about him was absolutely true when he said that he had seen him not living as he should in accordance with the true words of the gospel, and he very rightly told him that he was compelling the Gentiles to live like Jews. Paul was not guilty of this; he really did observe those ancient customs when obliged to in order to show that they ought not to be condemned and yet he was insistent in preaching that it was not by means of them but by the grace of faith revealed that the faithful would be saved and that no one should be compelled to observe them as necessary for salvation. I believe that in all he did the apostle Paul acted honestly, but I myself would not compel or even allow any Jewish convert to Christianity to perform such things sincerely, just as you who believe that Paul acted hypocritically in this matter would not compel or allow him to pretend to observe them.

Will you permit me to sum up your inquiry, or rather your opinion, thus: after the gospel of Christ Jewish Christians are right to offer sacrifices as Paul did and to circumcise their sons as Paul circumcised Timothy and to observe the sabbath as all the Jews did, as long as their actions are motivated by pretence and deceit.[35] If this is really so, we are now falling not into the Ebionite heresy or into that of the so-called Nazarenes or into any of the old heresies but into some new one which is all the more dangerous because it is not the result of error but is intentionally and voluntarily deceitful. You may try to show that you are not guilty of this by replying that at that time the apostles were right to pretend to do these things, to prevent the weaker Christians from being shocked, for there were many Jewish converts who did not yet understand that such practices should be rejected; but now that the doctrine of Christian grace has grown strong throughout so many countries, as has the reading of the law and the prophets in all the churches of Christ (although these are read for the sake of understanding, not for observance), any one who wishes to perform these things as a pretence is insane. Why should I not be allowed to say that the apostle Paul and other orthodox Christians were obliged at that time to observe those ancient traditions for a short while in order to show their sincere approval of them? Otherwise it might be thought that those observances of prophetic significance practised by their ancestors were detested by their descendants as sacrilegious and diabolical. For now, after the coming of the faith which had been prefigured in those observances and revealed after the death and resurrection of the Lord, these rituals had lost, as it were, their vital role. They had to be treated rather like the bodies of dead relatives which must be carried out for burial not as a matter of form but with true reverence; they were not to be abandoned immediately or exposed to the attacks of their enemies as to the teeth of dogs. But if any

Christian nowadays, even though he is a convert from
Judaism, should wish to perform these observances in
this way and as it were to stir up dead ashes, he will
not be behaving like a dutiful attendant or bearer of
the corpse but like some wicked violator of the tomb.

Of course I admit that with regard to what I said
in my letter[36] - that Paul agreed to observe the
Jewish rituals although he was already the apostle of
Christ, so as to show that they were not dangerous for
those wishing to observe them in the way they had
received them through the law from their fathers - I
should have added, 'at any rate at that time when the
grace of the faith was first revealed, for they were
not harmful then.' But after a certain period these
observances ought to have been abandoned by all
Christians; had they continued to be practised then it
would have been impossible to distinguish the
commandments which God had given his people through
Moses from the rites which the unclean spirit had
instituted in the temples of the demons. And it is
therefore my negligence, rather than your rebuke, which
is to blame if I failed to add this.

In fact, long before I received your letter, in my
work against Faustus the Manichee,[37] I did try to
explain this passage, albeit briefly, and then I did
mention this; you can read it yourself, if you wish,
and my dear friends, in whose hands I have now sent
these writings as you wanted, will also assure you,
whenever you want, that I did include this rider
before. I beg you by the obligations of friendship to
believe that I speak the truth when I say before God
that I never considered that Christian converts from
Judaism should nowadays perform those ancient rites,
whatever their feelings and intentions, or that they

should in any way be allowed to do so. I always
believed that Paul held this view, ever since I became
familiar with his letters; neither do you think that at
the present time anyone ought to pretend to do these
things, even though you believe that the apostles did
so.

On the other hand, in spite of the world's
protests, as you put it, you declare[38] that the
Jewish rituals are harmful and even deadly to
Christians and that anyone who practises them, whether
formerly a Jew or Gentile, is hurled down into the
devil's pit: I entirely agree with your words but
would add that anyone who performs them, whether
sincerely or with dissimulation, is cast into the
devil's pit. What more do you want? But just as you
make a distinction between the apostle's pretence and
contemporary procedure, so I distinguish between the
behaviour of the apostle Paul at that time, which I
believe was sincere on all points, and the Jewish rites
practised in our own day, however sincerely; for they
were permissible at that time but are now abhorrent.
It is true that it is written, 'The law and the
prophets down to John the Baptist' [Luke 16.16] and,
'The Jews sought to kill Christ not only because he
relaxed the sabbath regulations but because he even
said that his father was God, thereby making himself
equal to God' [John 5.18] and, 'We have received grace
upon grace for the law was given through Moses, while
grace and truth came to us through Jesus Christ' [John
1.16-17]; it is also true that through Jeremiah God
promised that he would give a new covenant to the house
of Judah, unlike the one which he had given to their
fathers.[39] Nevertheless, I do not think that the
Lord himself was circumcised by his parents as a

pretence or if he was too young to avoid circumcision,
I do not believe that he spoke deceitfully to the leper
who was cleansed not by the practices enjoined by Moses
but by the Lord himself who said to him, 'Go and offer
a sacrifice on your behalf which Moses commanded as a
testimony to them.'[40]          Nor was he acting
disingenuously when he went up to the feast day; he
only went up secretly rather than openly because he
wanted to avoid any ostentation in front of the
people.[41]

On the other hand, the same apostle said, 'Behold
I, Paul, say to you that if you are circumcised, Christ
will not benefit you at all.' [Gal. 5.2]  Did he then
deceive Timothy and make Christ useless to him?  Or was
it not harmful because it was done as a pretence?  But
that was not how he put it nor did he make any
distinction between those who were truly circumcised
and those who had had it done as a pretence, but
without making any exception he said, 'If you are
circumcised, Christ will not benefit you at all.'  And
so just as you wish your view to be accommodated and
you want the words 'except as a pretence' to be
understood, so I am justified in demanding that you
also allow me to understand that his words 'If you are
circumcised' applied to those who wanted to be
circumcised because they believed that otherwise they
could not be saved in Christ.  If it was in this frame
of mind, with this wish, with this intention that
someone ·at that period had himself circumcised, Christ
would not benefit him at all; Paul states this clearly
in another passage, 'For if righteousness comes by the
law, then Christ died to no purpose.' [Gal. 2.21]  He
also declares, as you yourself pointed out, that Christ
has become of no effect to those who are justified by

the law; they have fallen from grace.(42)   He was
criticising those who believed that they were justified
by the law, not those who were performing legitimate
practices out of respect for the one who had prescribed
these things; these people understood that they had
been prescribed as foretelling the coming of the truth
and that they should only continue to practise them
until such a time.  That is why he said, 'If you are
led by the Spirit, you are no longer under the law'
[Gal. 5.18]:   these words make it clear, as you can
see, that anyone who is under the law - not by way of
accommodation to the divine purpose,(43) as you think
our forbears believed, but in a literal sense which is
how I take it - does not possess the Holy Spirit.

I believe that it is important to find out in what
sense the apostle considers it reprehensible to be
under the law.   I do not think Paul was referring to
circumcision or to those sacred rites performed at that
period by our ancestors but not by Christians nowadays
or to things of this kind, but to the fact that the law
says, 'Do not covet' [Exod. 20.17], a commandment which
I admit that Christians must undoubtedly obey and
preach, putting it vividly to people as an essential
part of the Gospel.  Paul affirms that the law is holy
and that the commandment is holy and just and good and
then adds, 'Did then that which is good become death to
me? Of course not.   It was sin, working death in me
through what is good, in order that sin might be shown
to be sin, and through the commandment might become
sinful beyond measure.' [Rom. 7.13]  What he says here
about becoming sinful beyond measure through the
commandment, he expresses elsewhere when he says, 'The
law entered so that sin might abound.   But where sin
abounded, grace abounded all the more' [Rom. 5.20]; and

in another passage, after speaking first about the
previous dispensation of grace which justifies, he adds
a question, 'What then is the point of the law?',
immediately answering his own question by saying, 'It
was put into effect because of transgression until the
seed should come to whom the promise was made.' [Gal.
3.19] He says, then, that those are under the law in a
culpable manner whom the law has condemned for not
fulfilling the law, because they refuse to understand
the gift of grace and in their pride and arrogance
assume that they can carry out God's commandments by
their own efforts. But love is the fulfilment of the
law, and the love of God is poured forth in our hearts
not by ourselves but by the Holy Spirit which is given
to us. [Rom. 13.10, 5.5]

However, it would probably need a long discussion
and a special volume to give a satisfactory explanation
of this subject. If this commandment of the law - do
not covet - makes the man who is subject to it guilty
and condemns the sinner instead of freeing him, how
much less likely it is that justification should come
through those precepts which were merely figurative in
significance (i.e. circumcision and such like) and
which it was necessary to remove when the revelation of
grace spread further. But they were not to be shunned
as if they were the diabolic and sacrilegious practices
of the pagans, even after grace, which had been
prefigured by them, began to be revealed; instead they
were permissible for a short while, especially for
those who had come from that people to whom they had
been given. Afterwards, when they had been, as it
were, buried with honour, they had to be abandoned
unequivocally by all Christians.

When you say,[44]'not by way of accommodation to

the divine purpose, as our forbears believed,' please explain what you mean. For either it is what I would call a white lie[(45)] and this hypocrisy implies, a sort of duty to lie honestly, so to speak; otherwise I cannot understand what it can be, unless perhaps the addition of the phrase, 'by way of accommodation' means that a lie is no longer a lie. If you find this suggestion absurd, why do you not admit openly that a dutiful lie is defensible? Perhaps the word 'duty' disturbs you, seeing that it is not so common in ecclesiastical literature, although our friend Ambrose was not afraid to use it when he decided to call certain of his books, full of useful advice, 'On Moral Duties'.[(46)] If someone tells a lie out of a sense of duty is he to be blamed, while if he does so by way of accommodation is he to be approved? I ask you whether he who chooses one of these alternatives believes that one can lie; it is an important question whether it is sometimes permissible for a good man to lie, or rather whether it is permissible for a Christian to do so, to whom Christ said, 'Let your speech consist of "yes, yes" and "no, no" '[Matt. 5.37, James 5.12] and who heard with faith the psalmist say, 'You will lose all those who tell lies.' [Ps. 5.6/7] But, as I said, this is a different question - and an important one. Let him who believes that one can lie choose whichever justification he wants as long as it is firmly believed and maintained that the authors of the Holy Scriptures and especially of the canonical books are completely free from falsehood; otherwise the stewards of Christ, of whom it is said, 'It is required of stewards that each of them be found trustworthy' [1 Cor. 4.2], might believe that in learning that it is permissible to lie for the sake of truth, they had learned something important and in accordance with the faith. However, the Latin word 'fides' is derived from the phrase 'fit quod dicitur' (one does what one says)[47] and when one does what one says, there is of course no place for lying.

The apostle Paul who was a trusty steward undoubtedly reveals his honesty to us in his writings because he was a steward of the truth not of falsehood. And so he was telling the truth when he wrote that he had seen Peter not living as he should live in accordance with the true words of the gospel and had confronted him because he was compelling the Gentiles to live as Jews. As for Peter, he received with a devout, holy and good-natured humility the rebuke which Paul gave him for his benefit with the frankness of love.[48] In not refusing to be corrected by his inferiors he thus presented a rarer and more holy example to future generations when he happened to have wandered from the right path than Paul, who showed how those lower in authority may dare to stand firm in defending the truth of the gospel, as long as they do so with brotherly love. Although it is better, in following the path, not to deviate from it at all, it is, however, far more remarkable and praiseworthy to accept criticism cheerfully than to rebuke someone presumptuously when they have gone astray. As far as I can see from my limited viewpoint, it would have provided a better defence against Porphyry's criticisms to have praised Paul's fairness and outspokenness and Peter's humility, instead of giving Porphyry more opportunity for criticism, allowing him to accuse the Christians far more viciously of dishonesty in writing their letters or in performing their sacred rites.[49]

You demand that I name at least one person whose

opinion in this matter I have followed,[50] since you
have mentioned so many by name who have anticipated
your view on this question; and you ask that if I find
you to be at fault here, I should allow you to be at
fault in the company of such writers[51] - none of whom
I have read, I must admit. But of the approximately
six or seven whom you list, you undermine the authority
of four of them, for you admit that Apollinaris of
Laodicea, whose name you do not mention, has recently
left the Church, while Alexander was an old heretic,
and as for Origen and Didymus, I read that you have
criticised them severely in your more recent writings -
and on no trivial issues - even though you previously
praised Origen to a remarkable degree. I do not think
that you would allow yourself to share in these men's
errors, although in this passage you spoke as if they
had not been mistaken in their opinion. Who would wish
to be in error with someone of no importance? And so
there are only three left, Eusebius of Emesa, Theodore
of Heraclea and John, the one whom you mention a little
later, who was recently bishop at Constantinople.

Furthermore, if you should inquire or recall to
mind what our friend Ambrose's ideas on this subject
were or what Cyprian thought,[52] you might perhaps
find that I, too, have authors to follow with regard to
the opinion which I support. However, as I said a
little earlier, I owe such loyal submission only to the
canonical Scriptures; these alone do I follow with a
conviction that their authors made absolutely no
mistakes and wrote nothing to deceive me. But if I
have to look for a third author so as to confront your
three with three of my own, I could certainly, I think,
find one without difficulty, had I read widely. But
the apostle Paul presents himself to me as an

alternative to all these, or rather as superior to them
all. I take refuge with him and appeal to him against
all those commentators of his letters who hold a
different opinion; it is he whom I question and
interrupt, asking whether he wrote the truth or whether
because of some prudent dissimulation he was perhaps
lying when he wrote to the Galatians that he had seen
Peter not living as he should in accordance with the
true words of the gospel and had confronted him openly
because he was using this pretence to compel the
Gentiles to live as Jews.[53] I hear him calling out
to me in a solemn voice what he wrote a little earlier
at the beginning of this text, 'In what I am writing to
you - God is my witness - I do not lie.' [Gal. 1.20]

Anyone who holds a different opinion must forgive
me; I have more faith in this great apostle when he
takes an oath in defending his letters, than in any
other learned man discussing someone else's writings.
I am not afraid to have it said of me that I am
defending Paul by saying that he did not pretend to
hold the error of the Jews because he really did share
their error. Certainly he was not pretending to hold
their error when, with the apostolic frankness which
was fitting at the time, he gave those ancient rituals
the stamp of approval by performing them, to show that
they were established not by Satan's wiles to deceive
men but by God's providence as a prophecy to foretell
future events; but neither did he really share the
error of the Jews, for not only was he aware, but he
also repeatedly and vehemently stated, that they were
mistaken in thinking that these rituals had to be
imposed on the Gentiles or that they were necessary for
the justification of any believer.

I also said[54] that Paul became as a Jew to the

Jews and a Gentile to the Gentiles not with the cunning of a liar but with the love of one who feels compassion, but it seems to me that you did not pay sufficient attention to how I said it, or perhaps I was unable to explain it satisfactorily. I did not mean that he did these things as a pretence and out of pity, but that just as he was not pretending to conform to Jewish customs, neither was he pretending when he behaved like a Gentile, as you mentioned, thereby coming to my assistance, a fact I admit with gratitude. For when I asked you in my letter[55] how Paul could be understood to have become as a Jew to the Jews if he practised the Jewish rituals only as a pretence, although when he became as a Gentile to the Gentiles he did not pretend to perform any pagan rituals, you answered[56] that he became as a Gentile to the Gentiles in that he accepted uncircumcision and allowed them to eat without restriction foods which the Jews condemned. I therefore ask whether he did this also as a pretence; but if this is utterly absurd and wrong, then the same applies also to those things in which he conformed to the Jewish custom, acting with prudent independence rather than out of servile necessity, or what would have been more shameful, motivated by a diplomacy which was deceitful rather than sincere.

To the faithful and those who know the truth (as Paul himself bears witness, unless perhaps he is mistaken on this point also), everything created by God is good and nothing is to be rejected if it is received with gratitude [1 Tim. 4.4]. And so for Paul, too, not only as a man but as a particularly trustworthy steward[57] who both knew and taught the truth, everything created by God, at least as far as food is concerned, is really good, not just as a matter of pretence. Why then did he become as a Gentile to the Gentiles when he did not perform any of the pagan rites or ceremonies even in pretence, but believed and taught the truth about foods and about circumcision, although he was unable to become as a Jew to the Jews without pretending to accept the Jewish rites? Why did he save the ministry of the true faith for the grafted olive shoot while he spread some kind of veil of prudent dissimulation over the natural branches which had grown on the tree and were not introduced from outside?[58] Why when he became as a Gentile to the Gentiles did he teach what he believed and believe what he practised, but when he became as a Jew to the Jews he kept one thing shut up in his heart but expressed something different in his words, deeds and writings? Far be it from me to believe such a thing! To both parties he owed love which issues from a pure heart and a good conscience and sincere faith [1 Tim. 1.5], and that is how he became all things to all men so that he might benefit them all [1 Cor. 9.22], not with the cunning of a liar but with a feeling of compassion - in other words not by pretending to commit all the evil deeds of men but by diligently applying the medicine of compassion to the evil deeds of all other people as if they were his own. Consequently, in not refusing to perform those Old Testament rites he was not acting deceitfully out of pity - in fact he was not acting deceitfully at all; instead he was expressing approval for those things which had been commanded by the Lord God as relevant up to a certain point in his plan, thereby distinguishing them from the sacrilegious pagan rites. At that time, however, he became as a Jew to the Jews not with the cunning of a liar but with the love of one who feels compassion, for he wished to free them from the error which either made them unwilling to believe in Christ or made them think that they could be cleansed from their sins and be saved by means of their ancient priesthoods and by continuing to observe their traditional customs. He did so as if he himself were subject to that error, for he loved his neighbour as himself[59] and treated others as he wished others to treat him, if it was necessary; when the Lord gave this commandment he added, 'For this is what the law and the prophets amount to.' [Matt. 7.12]

In the same letter to the Galatians Paul commended this feeling of compassion when he wrote, 'If a man is caught in any wrong-doing, you who are spiritual should restore him in a spirit of gentleness, looking to yourself lest you yourself should be tempted.' [Gal. 6.1] Consider whether he did not mean that one should become like him so that one might benefit him, not of course by pretending to commit the same wrong or deceiving people into thinking one had committed it, but by seeing in another's sin what might happen to oneself also. In this way one could help the other person compassionately, just as one would want to be helped by him - in other words not with the cunning of a liar but with a feeling of compassion. In this way Paul became all things to all men so that he might benefit all[60] - the Jew, the Gentile and any man whatsoever who was involved in some error or sin; he did so not by pretending to be what he was not but by showing compassion because he too might find himself in the same position, knowing that he was a man like any other.

I ask you, please, to consider yourself and your attitude to me and recall to mind, or if you have them written down, reread the words you wrote in that rather

brief letter[61] which you gave to Cyprian, our brother
and now also our colleague, to deliver to me.  With
what feelings of sincere brotherly love you complained
that I had wronged you in certain ways and then added
ominously, 'By this means friendship is injured and the
bonds of intimacy are broken.  Let us not give the
impression that we are quarrelling childishly and give
our supporters or critics cause for dispute.'[62]  I
know that these words of yours were not only sincerely
spoken but also with kind intentions, for you have my
best interests at heart.  Then you add - and this would
be obvious even if you had not added it - that you are
writing this because you wish to love me in a pure and
Christian manner and not to harbour any thought which
is not in harmony with your words.  O you saintly man,
whom I love sincerely as God is my witness, I do not
doubt that the view you expressed in your letters is
the same as the one revealed by the apostle Paul in his
letters; I believe that he showed that he harboured no
thought in his mind which was not in harmony with his
words, and showed it not to one person in particular
but to the Jews and Greeks and all the Gentiles - the
sons whom he had fathered in the gospel or for whose
birth he was in labour[63] - and finally to all the
thousands of faithful Christians of later generations,
for  whose  sake  that  letter  was  handed  down  to
posterity.

I am sure that you also, like myself, acted not
with the cunning of a liar but with a feeling of
compassion when you thought that I should not be left
like this in the error into which you considered that I
had fallen, just as you yourself would not wish to be
left there if you had fallen into it.  I am grateful
for your kindness towards me but I also ask you not to

be offended with me for making known to you my
uneasiness with certain ideas expressed in your
writings. I wish everybody to treat me in the way I
have treated you; if they find anything in my writings
which they consider reprehensible, they should not keep
it dishonestly hidden in their heart nor criticise it
in front of others while they keep silent in my
presence, for I believe that it is this kind of
behaviour which is more likely to be destructive of
friendship. I do not know whether those friendships
are to be regarded as Christian in which the common
proverb, 'Flattery makes friends, truth makes
enemies',(64) is more applicable than the biblical one,
'The wounds of a friend are more trustworthy than the
calculated kisses of an enemy.' [Prov. 27.6]

Let us, then, make it clear to our dearest
friends, who support us wholeheartedly, that it is
possible for friends to disagree but that their love
for each other is not thereby diminished; honesty,
which should be part of friendship, does not
necessarily breed hatred, as long as the contrary
opinion - whatever it may be - is true and sincerely
expressed, without some thought being concealed which
is not in harmony with the words spoken. Our brothers,
your friends, to whom you bear witness that they are
the vessels of Christ, must believe that it was against
my will and a cause of great pain to me that my letter
came into the hands of many others before it could
reach you to whom it had been written. It would take
too long to explain how this happened, and, unless I am
mistaken, it is unnecessary to explain it; it is enough
if people believe me when I say that this did not
happen with the intention which people suppose and that
it was in no way my wish or my plan or with my

agreement that it happened: not only would I never have agreed to it, I never even dreamed that such a thing might happen. If they do not believe what I say with God as my witness, I do not know what more I can do. But far be it from me to think that they suggested this to you with malicious intent so as to arouse enmity between us - may the mercy of our Lord God keep such a thing from us - but even without there being any intention of harming it is easy to suspect faults which are only human in a man. It is fair that I should suppose that this was the case with them, if they are vessels of Christ, made not for shame but for honour and set up by God in a great house to be useful in his service.[65] But if, after this attestation of mine, should it come to their notice, they wish to do what is not right, you can see it for yourself.

What I wrote[66] about not having sent any book attacking you to Rome is true. I wrote this because I drew a distinction between the words 'book' and 'letter,' about which I thought that you had heard something completely different; I did not send that letter to Rome but to you and I did not think that I attacked you because I knew that I had written it in sincere friendship to advise you or to put you right or to be myself put right by you. But leaving aside your friends,[67] I beg you by that grace by which we are redeemed that whatever good things have been granted to you by the Lord in his goodness and which I referred to in my letter, you should not think that I mentioned them out of dishonesty to flatter you; but if I offended you in any way, forgive me. As for the passage, inspired by the fate of some poet or another which I recalled perhaps with more ineptness than wit, do not apply it to yourself more literally than I

intended, since I added immediately that I did not mean
that you should recover the eyes of your heart 'which
God forbid that you have lost,' I said, but that you
should take care to keep them healthy and watchful.[68]
I thought I ought to mention this story only because of
the palinode which we should imitate if we write
something which we are obliged to retract in a later
work, not because of Stesichorus' blindness which I
neither attributed to your heart nor feared for it.  I
ask you again and again to correct me boldly when you
see that I need it.  It is true that a bishop is
greater than a presbyter according to the current
terminology of ecclesiastical office, but Augustine is
still in many respects inferior to Jerome; but one
should not shrink from or scorn correction even from an
inferior.

On the question of your translation, you have now
persuaded me of your positive reasons for translating
the Scriptures from the Hebrew; you wanted to make
known to the public what had been left out or corrupted
by the Jews.  But I ask you, please, to inform me which
Jews did this - whether it was those who translated
before the coming of the Lord and if so, which ones, or
which one, or whether it was those later translators
who might be thought to have removed some things from
the Greek texts or to have corrupted them, in case they
should be refuted by the testimonies concerning the
Christian faith, (though I cannot see why those earlier
translators should have had any reason to do this).
Then please send me, I beg you, your translation from
the Septuagint which I was unaware that you had
published.[69]  I would also like to read that book of
yours which you mentioned, entitled 'The Best Method of
Translation'[70] and there is something else I wish to

know - how can a translator harmonise his linguistic skill with the conjectures of the systematic exegetes of the Scriptures? It is inevitable that even if they belong to the true and only faith, they will put forward many different opinions, given the obscurity of many passages, although this variety in no way conflicts with the unity of the faith; similarly, the obscurity of the text allows the commentator to explain one and the same passage in different ways without diverging from the true faith.

I am very keen to see your translation of the Septuagint as it will enable us to get away, as far as possible, from the terrible defects of the Latin translators who attempted this work whether qualified to do so or not. Those who think[71] that I am jealous of your useful labours might now at last understand, if they are able, that the reason I was unwilling for your translation from the Hebrew Bible to be read in the churches was that I wanted to avoid introducing it as something new and as a rival to the authority of the Septuagint, in case it should confuse the Christian congregation when their ears and hearts are used to this translation which even the apostles approved of. That is why if that shrub in the Book of Jonah is neither an ivy nor a gourd in the Hebrew version, but something else which leans on its own stem and grows without being supported by any prop, I would still prefer that 'gourd' be read in all the Latin versions, for I do not think that the Septuagint used this word without good reason: these translators must have known that this is more or less what it meant.[72]

I think I have written enough - perhaps more than enough - in reply to your three letters, two of which were brought to me by Cyprian and one by Firmus.[73]

Please write back telling me what you thought, so that
we or others can learn from it. For my part I will try
to make sure, with the Lord's help, that the letters I
write to you reach you before anyone else who might
circulate them further.(74) For I admit that I would
not wish this to happen to your letters to me and you
are quite right to complain about it. I hope that in
our relations there may exist between us not only the
affection but also the frankness due to friendship.
Neither of us should remain silent if we find anything
we object to in each other's letters but we must of
course express our criticisms in an attitude of
brotherly love which is pleasing to God. If you think
criticism is impossible without injury to love itself,
then we should not make it. The love which I hope can
exist between us is undoubtedly superior, but this
inferior love is better than nothing!

NOTES

1. Aug. Ep. 73.

2. Jer. Ep. 105.

3. Jer. Ep. 115.

4. Aug. Ep. 73.6-8.

5. In his Ep. 73 Augustine had written, 'I think that
through God's mercy I can easily beg you to forgive me
if I have offended you in any way.'

6. i.e. Aug. Ep. 73.

7. Cf. Jer. Ep. 115.

8. Cf. Jer. Ep. 102 where he wrote, 'It is a mark of childish boastfulness to seek fame for oneself by attacking illustrious men.'

9. Cf. Jer. Ep. 105 where he wrote, 'I did not believe that the letter nor the honey-coated sword were yours.' See note ad loc.

10. The canonical books were those which were regarded as divinely inspired; there was, however, disagreement about which books should rank as canonical. Augustine in his De Doctrina Christiana II.8.13 [CCL 32.39-40] gives a list of all the O.T. and N.T. books which he considers canonical and shows that he accepted all the books of the Septuagint as equally authoritative. Jerome, on the other hand, accepted only the books of the basic Hebrew canon and refused to accord the same status to the works which now usually appear in the Apocrypha of the Authorised and Revised Versions.

11. Cf. Jer. Ep. 102.2.

12. Cf. Gal. 4.19.

13. Cf. Matt. 26.69-75.

14. Cf. 2 Sam. 11.2-17.

15. Cf. Aug. Ep. 28.3.

16. We are informed of the Manichees' rejection of the Old Testament by remarks made by Augustine in his works De Genesi contra Manichaeos [P.L. 34], Contra Adminantum and Contra Faustum [CSEL 25]; cf. Jer. Ep. 112 n. 31 above. Of the New Testament they accepted only those parts which were not in manifest disagreement with their beliefs, rejecting anything which saw the N.T. in terms of a fulfilment of the O.T., as well as the accounts of Christ's infancy and passion; their version of the New Testament therefore seems to have comprised a mutilated part of the Gospels together with Paul's Epistles.

17. Jer. Ep. 112.4; Comm. in Gal. 2.11 [P.L. 26.339].

18. Cf. Aug. Comm. in Gal. 2.11 [P.L. 35.2114].

19. Cf. Acts 16.3, 18.18, 21.18-26.

20. Cf. Col. 2.17, Hebr. 10.1.

21. Acts 21.21.

22. Cf. Aug. cont. Faust. Manich. 19.17 [CSEL 25.1 pp. 514-516].

23. Cf. Acts 15.28.

24. Cf. Rom. 3.2.

25. Cf. Aug. cont. Faust. Man. 19.17 [CSEL 25.1 pp. 514-516].

26. Cf. Col. 2.17, Hebr. 10.1.

27. Acts 16.1-3.

28. Cf. Aug. Comm. in Gal. 2.3 [P.L. 35.2111].

29. Augustine is here referring to what Jerome wrote in his Ep. 112.

30. Cf. Jer. Comm. in Gal. 2.11 [P.L. 26.340].

31. Cf. John 14.6, 1 John 5.6.

32. Cf. Col. 2.17, Hebr. 10.1.

33. Cf. Ezech. 20.25.

34. In his Ep. 112 Jerome had implied that Augustine was guilty of the heresies of Cerinthus and the Ebionites in allowing those who had converted to Christianity to continue practising the Jewish law.

35. Augustine here ironically repeats almost word for word Jerome's rather pompous caricature of Augustine's argument; but in summarising Jerome's argument in this way Augustine adds the clause, 'as long as their actions are motivated by pretence and deceit,' thereby bringing out the absurdity of Jerome's view. Whereas Jerome had hinted that Augustine was guilty of the heresies of Cerinthus and of the Ebionites, Augustine here turns the tables on him and suggests that Jerome is himself guilty of some new heresy which imputes deceit to the apostles.

36. Aug. Ep. 40.4.

37. Aug. cont. Faust. Man. 19.17 [CSEL 25.1 pp. 514-516].

38. Jer. Ep. 112.14.

39. Jerem. 31.31.

40. Mc. 1.40-44.

41. Cf. John 7.10.

42. Cf. Gal. 5.4, Jer. Ep. 112.14.

43. In their dictionary Lewis and Short give the meaning of dispensative as used here as 'in the manner of an administrator, in substitution' which fails to bring out its connection with the divine dispensation.

44. Jer. Ep. 112.14.

45. Cf. Aug. 28.3.

46. The work referred to here is Ambrose's De Officiis Ministrorum [P.L. 16.23-184].

47. Augustine probably has in mind Cicero's De Officiis I.8.23 where he writes, 'And so we venture to follow the Stoics who are very interested in etymology, in accepting that faith is so called because what is promised is made good (fit quod dictum est).'

48. Cf. Aug. Comm. in Gal. 2.11 [P.L. 35.2114].

49. Cf. Jer. Ep. 112.11.

50. On Augustine's attitude to authority, see Brown passim; on the divine authority of Scripture, see Polman pp. 63-6.

51. Cf. Jer. Ep. 112.6 where he gives a list of authors whom he takes as authoritative.

52. Ambrose's ideas on the subject of Paul's rebuke of Peter are not known. For Cyprian's view, see his Ep. 71.3 [CSEL 3.2 pp. 773-4].

53. Cf. Gal. 2.11-14.

54. Cf. Aug. Ep. 40.6, Jer. Ep. 112.17.

55. In Ep. 40 Augustine had written to Jerome, 'If Paul took part in these rituals by pretending to be a Jew in order to win them over, why did he not also sacrifice with the Gentiles, putting himself outside

the law as they were outside the law, so that he might win them, too?

56. Jer. Ep. 112.17.

57. Cf. 1 Cor. 4.2.

58. Cf. Rom. 11.17.

59. Cf. Matt. 22.39.

60. Cf. 1 Cor. 9.22.

61. Jer. Ep. 105.

62. Jer. Ep. 105.4.

63. Cf. Gal. 4.19.

64. Terence *Andria* 68.

65. Cf. 2 Tim. 2.20, Rom. 9.21.

66. Aug. Ep. 67.2.

67. Cf. Jer. Ep. 105.2.

68. Cf. Aug. Ep. 40.7.

69. Jerome refers to his translation of the Septuagint in his Ep. 134 to Augustine.

70. i.e. Jer. Ep. 57 to Pammachius [CSEL 54.503-526].

71. Cf. Jer. Ep. 105.2.

72. Cf. Jer. Ep. 112.22.

73. i.e. Jer. Ep. 105, Ep. 112 and Ep. 115.

74. Cf. Jer. Ep. 105.5.

AUGUSTINE EP. 166

I have prayed and continue to pray to our God who has called us to his kingdom and his glory [1 Thess. 2.12] that he may grant that what I write to you may be fruitful to me, my holy brother Jerome, when I consult you about matters of which I am ignorant. It is true that you are much older than me but even I am now an old man; however, I believe that one is never too old to learn what is necessary because even if it is more fitting for old men to teach than to learn, it is nevertheless better for them to learn than to teach things they do not know. In fact, there is nothing I find so hard to bear in all the perplexities which I experience in dealing with these very difficult problems than the absence of your fellowship and the great distance between us, which means that I can hardly reach you with my letters or receive yours within the space not of days or months but of several years. If only it were possible, I would like to have you with me every day so that I could talk to you on whatever subject I wished. But even if I cannot do everything I wish, I ought still to do what I can.

There came to me just now a devout young man, a brother in the Catholic faith, in age my son but in worthiness my fellow presbyter; he is Orosius,[1] a man with an alert mind, ready eloquence and burning with eagerness to be a useful instrument in the house of the Lord[2] for he longs to be able to refute the false and dangerous doctrines which are slaughtering the souls of the Spanish in a more terrible way than the barbarian sword slaughters their bodies.[3] He has hastened to come here right from the Atlantic coast, stimulated by the report that he could hear from me whatever he wanted of those topics in which he was interested. He did indeed derive some benefit from coming; first of all, he learned that he should not believe everything he was told about me; secondly, I taught the man what I could and told him where he could learn what I was unable to teach him; I also encouraged him to visit you. He willingly and obediently accepted my advice, or if you like, my command on this point, and so I asked him to visit me on his way back home from you. He gave me his promise, and so I believe that the Lord granted me this opportunity to write to you on the subject about which I want to learn from you. For I was looking for someone to send to you but it was not easy to find someone suitable who was reliable and keen to obey as well as an experienced traveller. When I got to know this young man, I could not doubt that he was exactly the sort of person I was asking for from the Lord.

I shall now tell you what I want you to explain to me - please take the trouble to deal with this question. The problem of the soul is one which bothers many people and I admit that I am one of them. I will state what I believe with certainty about the soul and then add what I would like to have explained to me. Man's soul is immortal in some special way of its own; it is not immortal in every respect as God is, of whom it is said that he alone possesses immortality.[4] In fact Holy Scripture makes many references to the death of the soul, for example, 'Let the dead bury the dead.' [Matt. 8.22, Luke 9.60] It dies when it is separated from the life of God, but it does so in such a way that it does not entirely cease to exist in its own essence.

Consequently it is found to be mortal from one point of view but can also not unreasonably be called immortal. The soul is not a part of God, for if it were, it would be entirely immutable and incorruptible, and it could neither deteriorate nor progress; it would not begin to have anything in itself which it did not have before and it would not cease to possess what it used to have, as far as its own feelings are concerned. There is no need of external proof to show that such a description would be most inaccurate; anyone who looks into himself can recognise this. It is useless for those who wish the soul to be a part of God[5] to say that the vileness and depravity of the soul which we see in wicked people and the weakness and disease which we recognise exists in all men are derived not from the soul but from the body. What difference does it make what the source of the disease is? If the soul were immutable, it could not possibly become diseased, for something which is truly immutable and incorruptible cannot be changed or corrupted by contact with any thing whatsoever. Otherwise it would not only be Achilles, as the myths relate, who was vulnerable, but all flesh, for no accident could befall it. The soul is therefore not immutable by nature since it is subject to change in some way, for some reason, in some part. On the other hand, we are not permitted to believe that God is anything but truly and supremely immutable, therefore the soul is not a part of God.

Although it can be difficult to convince those who are rather slow of understanding that the soul is not corporeal, I profess that I am convinced. But I do not wish to discuss the terminology unnecessarily or have such a discussion forced on me, for when there is agreement about a subject there is no need to argue about the terms; if the word 'body' means any substance or essence or whatever better word there may be to express the concept of something which in some way exists in itself, then the soul is a body. Similarly if one chooses to use the term incorporeal only of a nature which is utterly immutable and everywhere complete, then the soul is a body for it does not have these characteristics. However, if a thing is not a body unless it exists and moves in three dimensions in such a way that it occupies a larger space with a larger part of itself and a smaller space with a smaller part and that a part of it is less than its whole, then the soul is not a body. For the soul extends throughout the whole body to which it gives life, not by a distribution in space but by means of a sort of life-giving tension; it is completely present simultaneously throughout all its parts and it is not smaller in the smaller parts and larger in the larger parts, but in one place it exists more intensely, in another less so, and the whole of it exists in each and every part. Otherwise it would be impossible for the whole soul to feel what is not felt in the whole body; for when the living flesh receives a small prick, even though this spot not only does not extend over the whole body but is even hardly visible on the body, the whole soul still notices it, even when the feeling does not spread through all the parts of the body but is only perceived at the point where it is pricked.

How then does something which does not affect the whole body quickly reach the whole soul, if it is not because the whole soul exists at the point where the body is affected and does not need to abandon the rest of the body in order to be wholly present at that point? The other parts live because the soul is present, even where nothing of this kind has occurred. But if this did happen and both happened at the same time, then the whole soul would experience both at the same time. And so the soul could not exist as a whole in all the parts of the body and in each individual part simultaneously if it were extended through them in the way we see bodies extended in space, occupying smaller areas with their smaller parts and larger areas with their larger ones. That is why if the soul is to be called a body, it is certainly not a body in the way things are which are made of earth or water, air or ether,[6] for all these are larger if they occupy larger areas and smaller if they occupy smaller ones: none of them is entirely present in each of its parts but each part of space is occupied by a part of the body. It should therefore be understood that the soul, whether it is called a body or not, has a nature peculiar to itself created from a substance more excellent than all these elements of earthly matter; it cannot be accurately conceived in terms of physical images which we perceive by means of the senses, but is understood by the mind and perceived in living. I am not saying this to tell you things which you already know, but to show you what I firmly believe about the soul, so that when I come to those points which I want to ask you about, no one will think that I do not have any ideas, whether based on knowledge or faith, about the soul.

I am also certain that the soul fell into sin through no fault of God's, without any compulsion in itself or from God, but through its own will;[7] it cannot be freed from the body doomed to this death[8] by the strength of its own will as if it were self-sufficient or by the death of the body but by the grace

of God through Jesus Christ our Lord. There is not a
single human soul for whose freedom the man Christ
Jesus, the mediator of God and man [1 Tim. 2.5]., is not
needed. Any soul which departs from the body, at
whatever age, without the mediator's grace and without
his sacrament, will be punished and will, at the last
judgement, receive a body for punishment. But if,
after its human birth (which has taken place from the
time of Adam), it is reborn in Christ by belonging to
his followers, it will have rest after the death of the
body and will receive a body in which to share in
Christ's glory. This is what I firmly believe about
the soul.

Now please listen to what I am asking and do not
scorn me, so that he who condescended to be scorned for
us may not scorn you. My question is: where has the
soul contracted that guilt by which it is condemned,
even if it is the soul of an infant who died
prematurely, unless helped by Christ's grace, conferred
through the sacrament of baptism which even tiny babies
undergo. You are not one of those who have begun to
babble new ideas,[9] saying that in the case of an
infant there is no guilt inherited from Adam which has
to be removed by baptism. If I knew that you thought
this, or rather, if I did not know that you did not
think this, I would certainly not seek an answer from
you or think that it could be asked. But I am certain
that your opinion on this issue is in line with the
fundamental doctrines of the Catholic faith, because
when you cited this passage from the book of Job as
testimony to refute Jovinian's nonsense[10] - 'No one
is clean in your sight, not even an infant whose life
on earth lasts only a day' [Job 14.4] - you added, 'We
are considered guilty, as Adam was for his

transgression' [Rom. 5.14], and in your book on the
prophet Jonah you made this very clear when you said
that it was right for small babies to be forced to fast
because of original sin.[11] It is therefore quite
fitting for me to inquire of you where the soul
contracted this guilt, from which, even at that tender
age, it has to be released by means of the sacrament of
Christian grace.

In fact, a few years ago, when I was writing some
books on free will,[12] copies of which passed through
many hands and which a large number of people possess,
I put forward four views of the soul's incarnation for
discussion: whether all souls are created from that
one soul which was given to the first man or whether
new ones are being made even now for each individual;
or if they already exist somewhere, are they sent down
by God or do they fall into bodies of their own accord?
I wanted to treat these views in such a way that
whichever of them was true, it would not interfere with
my purpose at that time of opposing with all my might
those who attempt to introduce as God's opponent an
independent principle of evil. These were the
Manichees - for I had not yet heard of the
Priscillianists who invent blasphemous stories not very
different from theirs. I did not add the fifth view
which you mentioned amongst others, not wanting to omit
any from your letter to Marcellinus,[13] that man of
pious memory who was so dear to us in Christ's love and
who consulted you about this problem. According to
this view the soul is a part of God, but I did not
mention it firstly because the question under
discussion referred not to the soul's incarnation but
to its nature, and secondly because that is the view
held by those against whom I was arguing, and I was

particularly concerned to distinguish between the blameless and inviolable nature of the creator and the vices and defects of the creature, because the Manichees claim that the substance of evil, to which they attribute its own principle and powers, has corrupted and oppressed a part of the substance of the good God and forced it to sin. And so, omitting this erroneous and heretical view, I wish to know which one of the four remaining views I should choose. Whichever one is preferable, God forbid that it should contradict this article of faith of which we are certain, that every soul, even that of a tiny baby, needs to be delivered from the bond of sin and that this deliverance can only be effected by Jesus Christ and in Christ crucified.[14]

But to cut this account short: you, at any rate, are firmly convinced that God even now makes a separate soul for each individual as it is born. In answer to the possible objection that God finished making all creatures on the sixth day and on the seventh he rested, you adduce as proof the words of the Gospel, 'My Father is still working even now.' [John 5.17] This is what you wrote to Marcellinus and in that letter you were kind enough to mention me, pointing out that Marcellinus had me with him here in Africa and that it would be easier for me to give him an explanation of this subject.[15] If I had been able to do so, he would not have asked you for an answer to this problem as you live so far away - if indeed he really did write to you from Africa. I do not know when he wrote; I only know that he was well aware of my doubts on this subject which was why he was unwilling to consult me. However, even if he had consulted me, I would have encouraged him to write to you and would

have been grateful for the favour granted to us all.
But you preferred to write a brief reply rather than to
answer him at length. I suppose you did not want to
waste your effort since I was here and you thought I
knew best the answer to his problem. To be sure, I
would like this opinion to be mine also but I declare
that it is not yet so.

You sent me some students so that I should teach
them something I have not yet learned myself. Teach
me, then, what I should teach them; for many people are
demanding that I teach them but I confess to them that
I am as ignorant on this point as I am on many others.
And perhaps, although they are ashamed to say so to my
face, they say to each other, 'You are a master in
Israel and yet you do not know this' [John 3.10], which
is of course what the Lord said to that man who was one
of those who liked to be called Rabbi: perhaps the
reason why he came at night to the true master was that
he was ashamed to learn because he had been accustomed
to teach. But I prefer to listen to a master than to
be listened to as a master. I remember what Christ
said to those whom he chose in preference to all
others, 'Do not allow yourselves to be called Rabbi,
for Christ is your only master' [Matt. 23.8]. It was
none other who taught Moses, not even Jethro,[16] none
other who taught Cornelius through Peter who was the
chief apostle[17] and none other who taught Peter
through Paul,[18] his successor: anyone who speaks the
truth does so through him who is truth itself.[19]
Might it not be that if we are as yet ignorant of these
matters and have been unable to find an answer to them
through prayer or by reading, by reflection or reasoned
argument, it is because we are being tested to see not
only with what love we teach the ignorant but also with

what humility we learn from the learned?

And so I ask you to teach me what I should teach, teach me what I should believe and tell me, if souls are individually made even nowadays for each person as he is born, when do they sin as tiny babies to make them need remission from sin in Christ's sacrament? Is it because they have sinned in Adam from whom the flesh of sin is derived by generation? Or if they do not sin, how can it be just for the creator to hold them guilty of someone else's sin, when they are implanted into human bodies generated subsequently, with the result that although it is not in their power to be helped by the grace of baptism, they are damned unless they receive a remedy through the Church? How can it be fair that so many thousands of souls which, when tiny children die, depart from the body without the remission granted by the Christian sacrament should be damned, if they are created new by the will of the creator without any pre-existent sin on their part, each one clinging to the body of an individual at the moment of birth? Was he not aware that each one of these souls which he created and placed in the body to give it life would depart from the body with no sin of its own but without the baptism of Christ? It is obvious that we cannot say that God forces souls to become sinful or that he punishes them if they are innocent; nor are we allowed to deny that those souls which depart from their bodies without Christ's sacrament, even those of small children, are dragged to damnation.

I ask you, then, how can we defend the opinion which holds that all souls are not made from that of the first man but are created separately for each individual, just as that first one was? I think I can easily refute the other arguments put forward against this view, for example the one, thought forceful by some, which asks how God could have completed all his works on the sixth day and on the seventh have rested,[20] if he is still creating new souls? If we were to answer such people by quoting the passage from the Gospel which you cited in your above-mentioned letter, 'My Father is still working' [John 5.17], they will answer that 'working' refers to the administration of things which have already been made, not to the creation of new things; otherwise they would be contradicting the text of Genesis where it is clearly stated that God had finished making all his works. For if it is written that he rested, this must undoubtedly be understood as rest from creating new creatures, not from governing them. During those six days he made the things which did not exist and after making them he rested because he had completed everything whose existence he had foreseen before they existed; afterwards he created and made not things which did not exist but which were derived from those things which existed previously. This is how they show that both statements are true, both 'he rested from his works' [Gen. 2.2] and 'he is still working' [John 5.17], since the Gospel cannot contradict Genesis.

There are people who make this objection because they do not believe that God now makes new souls which did not previously exist, as when he created that first soul, but that he creates them from that one which already existed and sends them forth as from some source or treasury which he made at that time; but we can easily answer them by saying that even during those six days God created many things out of those natures which he had already created, for example birds and fishes from the waters and trees, grass and animals from the earth. But it is clear that at that time he made those things which did not yet exist: for there were no birds, no fishes, no trees, no animals, and one can easily understand that he rested after he had created these things which had not existed and which he created, in other words, he stopped creating any more creatures which did not yet exist. But now if we reject the view that he sends down souls already existing in some kind of store or that he sprinkles them with something of himself as if they were parts of him or that they are derived from that original soul or that he fetters them in the chains of a body as a punishment for sins committed before their incarnation, and if we say that he creates new ones individually for each person who is born, we are not saying that he is creating something which did not previously exist. Already on the sixth day he made man in his own image,(21) and this should of course be understood to refer to the rational soul. Even nowadays he does this not by creating what did not exist but by multiplying what already exists. And so it is true that he rested after creating things which had not existed but it is also true that he is even now working, not only by directing what he made but also by creating in greater numbers not things which he had not yet created but things which he had already made. By means of some such argument we can remove the objection made to us about God's rest after finishing his work which might hinder us from believing that new souls are still being made in the same way as that original soul rather than being derived from it.

As for the objection, 'Why does God make souls for those whom he knows will soon die?' we can answer that in this way the sins of the parents are made known or punished. We can with good reason leave these things to God's guidance, for we know that to all things which pass through time, such as living creatures which are born and die, he gives a beautifully ordered course: we cannot perceive this ourselves, but if we could, we would experience an ineffable joy. It was not in vain that the prophet who taught that his words were divinely inspired referred to God as the one who brings forth their host by number [Isa. 40.26]. That is why music, which is the understanding and feeling of rhythm, has been granted by God's munificence also to mortals who have rational souls so as to make them aware of this wonderful fact. A man who is a skilled composer knows what length to assign to each tone to make the melody flow and progress beautifully as a series of ascending and descending notes; is not God, whose all-creating wisdom far surpasses all skills, far more capable of allowing no moment of time (for moments are, as it were, the syllables and words of time) to pass more quickly or more slowly in this wonderful song, so to speak, of declining things, than the melody, foreknown and prescribed beforehand, demands. If this is true even of the leaves of the trees and the number of hairs on our heads, is it not all the more true of the birth and death of man? For man's temporal life only continues for as long a period as God, who controls time, knows will be in harmony with the order of the universe.

Some say that anything which has its starting point in time cannot be immortal because 'all things born must die and anything which grows must age',[22] wishing to force people to believe that the human soul is immortal only because it was created before all time, but they do not convince me. For the immortality of Christ's flesh, to mention no other argument, had its beginning in time but 'that will not now die and death will have no dominion over it' [Rom. 6.9].

As for what you wrote in your book against Rufinus[23] - that some people criticise this view unfairly because they believe it is unworthy of God to give souls to those conceived in an adulterous relationship, and that is why they attempt to claim that souls can justly be put into bodies as if into prisons because of their conduct in a life lived before their incarnation - I do not find this convincing; I can think of many ways of refuting this false claim.[24] You yourself replied that in the case of stolen wheat, the fault lies not in the sowing of the wheat but in the one who stole it; one cannot say that the earth ought not to have nourished the seeds in her belly, just because the sower scattered the seeds with a dirty hand. This is a most attractive comparison. Even before I had read it, this objection about those conceived in adultery did not present any problems to me, for in general I considered that God brings much good even from vices and bad things. But if the creation of every living creature inspires the good and wise man with unspeakable praise for the creator, is this not much more true of the creation, not of any ordinary living creature, but of man? If one is looking for the reason for this creation, there is no better or more ready answer than that since all God's creatures are good, what is more fitting than that a good God should create good things which no one apart from him can make?

These are the sort of arguments I use, according to my abilities, against those who try to undermine the

belief that souls are made for each individual as was
that of Adam.[25]   But when I come to the suffering of
infants I find myself struggling with enormous
problems, believe me, and I have no idea what to say -
I do not mean just those sufferings which damnation
brings after this life and which it is necessary for
them to be subjected to if they depart from the body
without the sacrament of Christian grace, but also
those which clearly exist in this life to our sorrow,
so numerous that if I wished to mention them all, I
would run out of time before I ran out of examples.
Children waste away through illness, they are tormented
by pain, they suffer agony through hunger and thirst,
their limbs are debilitated, they are deprived of their
faculties, they are harassed by unclean spirits.   It
certainly needs to be proved that it is just for them
to suffer all this, without any fault of their own, for
we cannot say that these things happen without God's
knowledge or that he is unable to resist whatever
causes them or that he causes them or allows them to
happen unjustly.   Could we properly say about man what
we say about irrational animals?   That they are granted
for use to superior natures, even wicked ones:   for
example, we see clearly in the Gospel that the pigs
were granted to the demons to be used as they wished.
Though man is an animal, he is a rational one, even
though mortal, and his soul which seems to suffer such
terrible afflictions as a punishment in those limbs, is
rational,  God is good, God is just, God is omnipotent
- only a complete madman would doubt this; and so a
just cause must be found for the great suffering of
small children.   To be sure, when adults suffer similar
things we usually say, as in the case of Job, that
their virtue is being tested, or as in the case of

Herod, that their sins are being punished; and from certain examples which God wished should be manifest it has been granted to men to make conjectures about others which are obscure. But this is in the case of adults. Please tell me what we should answer in the case of infants, if they have no sins which must be punished by means of such terrible suffering (for at that age they certainly have no virtue which needs to be tested).

And what should I say about diversity of intelligence? It does of course remain hidden in infants but develops from its natural beginnings[26] and manifests itself in older children, some of whom are so slow and forgetful that they are unable to attain even basic literacy, while others are so stupid that they are no different from animals - these are commonly referred to as morons. The answer might perhaps be that this diversity is caused by the body, but did the soul then, according to the view which we wish to defend, make a mistake when it came to choosing a body for itself and go wrong as a result? Or when it was forced to enter a body by the necessity of being born, could it find no other one because of the crowds of souls jostling to take possession of the other available bodies and so, like someone looking for a seat at a theatre, ended up taking not the body it wanted but whatever it could find?[27] Can we say such things or even think them? Tell me then what I should think and say so that our theory of the new souls individually made for each body may be proved correct.

In fact, in the books I wrote about free will I did say something, not about the intelligence of small children but about the suffering they endure in this life. I will give you an idea of what I said and why it is insufficient for the present question by quoting a passage from the third book[28] which reads, 'With regard to the torments of the body endured by small children who, because of their age, have no sins of their own, if the souls which give them life had no existence before the people themselves, there is room for a more serious complaint to be made - one which appears to be motivated by compassion. People say, "What wrong have they done that they should suffer like this?" as if there could be any merit in innocence before a person is capable of doing anything wrong! But when God does something for beneficial purposes and corrects adults by punishing them through the sufferings and death of their little children whom they love, why should this not happen, for once it is past, it will be as if it had never happened for those who suffer, while those for whose sake the sufferings occurred will either be better (if, admonished by such temporal tragedies, they choose to lead a better life) or when they come to be punished at the last judgement will have no excuse if they have refused to turn their thoughts away from the sufferings of this life towards eternal life. But who knows what special compensation God is reserving in the secrets of his judgements for those little children whose torments serve to break down the hardness of the adults or to test their faith or prove their compassion? For although the children have done nothing good, yet they have not sinned in any way even though they suffer such things; it is not without reason that the Church recommends that even those infants who were murdered when Herod was seeking to kill our Lord Jesus Christ should be received and honoured as martyrs.'

I wrote this at that time because I wanted to give

support to this particular view which we are now discussing. As I mentioned a little earlier, whichever of these four beliefs about the incarnation of the soul is true, the creator's substance is without blame and as far removed as possible from association with our sins: this is what I was trying to show. That was why I was not then concerned to prove which one of the four beliefs was true and which were to be rejected, for when all the views had been carefully discussed, whichever one prevailed over the others, I would feel quite secure because I had proved that according to each one of them the point I was making remained irrefutable. But now I wish, if possible, to choose one of the four as the correct explanation, because when I look more carefully at the passage I quoted from my book, I can find no strong, unshakeable defence of the view now being discussed. What I said above provides the basis of this view, so to speak: 'But who knows what special compensation God is reserving in the secrets of his judgements for those little children whose torments serve to break the hardness of the adults or to test their faith or prove their compassion?' But I realise that this could also apply to the children who suffer something similar even without knowing it for the sake of Christ and true religion or to those who have already been baptised with Christ's sacrament, because without belonging to the one mediator they cannot be released from damnation; and so the same compensation could be awarded to them, too, for the sufferings endured through the manifold afflictions of this life. But now, (since this problem cannot be solved unless an answer is also found to the question of the small children who suffer terrible torments and breathe their

last without the sacrament of the Christian community),
what compensation can be imagined for them for whom, in
addition to all the other sufferings, damnation is
waiting? In that book I provided some kind of
explanation about the baptism of small children - not,
it is true, an adequate one, but one that seemed
sufficient for that work: I said that baptism is of
benefit even to those who are ignorant and do not yet
have faith of their own, but I did not think anything
needed to be said at that point about the damnation of
those children who depart this life without baptism,
because I was not then concerned with the subject of
our present discussion.

However, if we do not mention or make much of the
sufferings they endure for a short while and which,
once past, are forgotten, can we similarly neglect the
fact that by one man came death and by one man the
resurrection of the dead? For as in Adam all die, even
so in Christ all are made alive. [1 Cor. 15.21-2] From
this divine and clear statement by the apostle it is
evident that no one has access to eternal life except
through Christ.(29) (That is no doubt what the two
uses of the word 'all' refer to, because just as all
men belong to Adam through their first, that is
physical, birth, so all men who come to Christ
experience a second, spiritual birth. That is why the
word 'all' is used in both places, because just as all
men who die do not die unless in Adam, so all who are
made alive are only made alive in Christ.) And so
anyone who tells us that a person can be made alive at
the resurrection of the dead except in Christ, deserves
to be detested as destructive of our common faith.
Similarly if anyone says that even small children who
depart this life without participating in Christ's

sacrament will be made alive, he is certainly
contradicting the teaching of the apostle and
condemning the whole Church, which hastens to baptise
tiny infants because it firmly believes that otherwise
they cannot possibly be made alive in Christ. As for
those who are not made alive in Christ, we must
conclude that they remain subject to that condemnation
of which the apostle says, 'One man's sin led to
condemnation for all men.' [Rom. 5.18] The whole
Church believes that tiny babies are born guilty of
this sin and you yourself in your argument against
Jovinian(30) and in your commentary on the prophet
Jonah,(31) as I mentioned a little earlier, stated this
clearly with true faith (I believe that you have done
so also in other passages in your works which I have
either not read or which I do not remember for the
moment.) It is the reason for this condemnation which
I seek to know, because if new souls are individually
made for each person I can see no sin in their souls at
that age and I do not believe that God condemns any
soul in which he sees no sin.

Perhaps we have to say that in a small child it is
only the flesh which is sinful but that a new soul is
made for it which, if it lives according to God's
commands with the help of Christ's grace, can obtain
the reward of incorruption even for the flesh, if this
is controlled and subdued. But because the soul of a
small child cannot yet do this, if it has received the
sacrament of Christ, it acquires for its flesh by means
of this grace what it cannot yet acquire by its own
virtuous behaviour; if however the child's soul departs
without that sacrament, will it share in eternal life
from which no sin can separate it, while its body will
not rise again in Christ because it had not received

his sacrament before death? This is not an opinion which I have ever heard or read, but this I certainly have heard and believed and have even spoken out in support of,[32] namely that a time will come when all who are in their graves will hear his voice, and those who have done good will proceed to the resurrection of life [John 5.28-9]; it is to this opinion which the passage, 'And by one man came the resurrection of the dead' refers, according to which all will be made alive in Christ [1 Cor. 15.21-2], while those who have done evil will proceed to the resurrection of judgement [John 5.29].

What then ought we to think about those infants who depart from the body without baptism before they are capable of either good or evil? Nothing is said about them here. If their flesh will not rise again because they have done neither good nor evil, then neither will the bodies of those who have died after receiving the grace of baptism at an age when they were unable to behave either morally or immorally rise again. If however the baptised rise again among the saints, in other words among those who have done good, among whom will those others be resurrected, if not among those who have done evil? Otherwise we should have to believe that some human souls will not receive their bodies either at the resurrection of life or at the resurrection of judgement. Even before this view is refuted, its very novelty makes it repellent. Furthermore, would it not be insupportable if those who came running with their tiny babies to baptism believed that they needed to hurry for the sake of their bodies rather than their souls? In fact, St. Cyprian was not decreeing anything new but was preserving a firmly held belief of the Church,[33] so as to correct those who thought that a baby must not be baptised until at least eight days after its birth, when he said that it was not the body but the soul which must be saved and decreed that a newly-born child could validly be baptised - a view which he shared with a number of his fellow bishops.

Each person can think what he likes - even if he disagrees with Cyprian who did not perhaps see things as he ought; but let no one hold an opinion contrary to the most evident faith of the apostle who preaches that from one man's sin all are subject to condemnation and only the grace of God through Jesus Christ our Lord can release us from this condemnation, for in Christ alone are all made alive who are made alive; let no one hold an opinion which conflicts with the firmly established custom of the Church, for if people hurried to bring babies to baptism for the sake of their bodies alone, even the dead could be brought forward for baptism. Since we hold this belief, we must look for and state the reason why, in the case of small children who die without Christ's sacrament, their souls are damned if a new one is created for each individual as it is born. Both Holy Scripture and the holy Church witness to the fact that they are damned if they depart from the body in this state,[34] and I will adopt the aforesaid view about the creation of new souls if it does not conflict with this most firmly founded belief; but if it does conflict, then you should not hold it.

I do not want anyone to tell me that we ought to take the passages where it says, 'He who made the spirit of man in him' [Zech. 12.1] and 'He who made their hearts one by one' [Ps. 32.15 (33.15)] as supporting this view. An extremely cogent and irrefutable argument is needed which does not force us

to believe that God condemns a soul without any guilt
on its part. For it is just as great or perhaps even
greater to create than to form and yet it is written,
'Create in me a clean heart, O God' [Ps. 50.12
(51.10)].(35) It cannot be thought that in this
passage the soul is asking to be made before it exists
at all. Just as the soul, already existing, is created
by a renewal of justice, so also, once it already
exists, it is formed by the shaping force of doctrine.
Nor does that passage from the book of Ecclesiastes,
'Then dust is turned into earth as it was and spirit
returns to the Lord who gave it' [Eccles. 12.7] confirm
this view which we wish to hold; it rather supports
those who think that all souls are derived from one.
For just as dust, they say, returns to earth where it
was before (although the flesh, which is here meant,
does not return to the man from whom it originally
came, but to earth from which the first man was made),
so also the spirit, derived from the spirit of that
first individual, does not return to him but to the
Lord who gave it to him. But because this testimony
supports their view without seeming completely contrary
to the view which I wish to defend, I believe that you
should merely be advised of the fact in case you should
use such testimony to try to rescue me from my
difficulties. Although no one can, simply by wishing,
make what is not true true, I would wish this opinion
to be true if it were possible, just as I wish that, if
it is true, you could defend it unequivocally and
irrefutably.

But this is a difficulty which besets even those
who believe that souls, already existing somewhere else
and prepared at the beginning of the divine works, are
sent by God into bodies. For one can put the same

question to them - if innocent souls go obediently to their destination, why are they punished in tiny children whose lives end without baptism? Exactly the same difficulty is present in both views. Those who assert that each soul is united to an individual body according to its merit in a former life believe that they can avoid this difficulty more easily. They think that to die in Adam means to pay the penalty in the flesh which has been generated from Adam; it is from this guilt, they say, that the grace of Christ frees both tiny children and adults. Indeed it is right, true and excellent to say that the grace of Christ frees both tiny children and adults from the guilt of their sins but I do not believe, do not accept, do not agree that the souls sinned in another earlier life and were then thrown into prisons of flesh: firstly, because I can think of no opinion more horrible than the complicated argument that after an unknown number of cycles of ages[36] one has to return to this burden of corruptible flesh and pay the penalty; secondly, if they are right, is there any virtuous person about whom, after his death, we ought not to worry that he might sin even in Abraham's bosom and be hurled down into the flames like that rich man?[37] Why should it be impossible to sin after life in this body if it was possible before it? Finally, it is one thing to have sinned in Adam, which is why the apostle says, 'In whom all have sinned' [Rom. 5.12], and something very different to have sinned somewhere outside Adam and as a result to be thrust into Adam, in other words into the flesh which is born from Adam, as if into a prison. I do not wish to discuss the view that all souls are derived from one original unless it is necessary, and I wish that if the opinion we are now discussing is true, it may be defended by you in such a way that this should no longer be necessary.

Although I wish and ask and pray most ardently and expect that through you the Lord will remove my ignorance on this matter, if I do not deserve it - and God forbid that this should be the case - I pray that the Lord our God will be patient with me; I have such faith in him that I ought not to murmur against him in any way if he does not open for us even when we knock. I remember what was said to the disciples themselves, 'I have many things to say to you but you cannot take them all in now.' [John 16.12] As far as I am concerned, this applies to my present difficulties and as I am aware of it, I would not be offended if I were regarded as unworthy, in case such an attitude on my part might prove me to be even more unworthy. There are many other things of which I am equally ignorant - I could neither count nor list them all. I would put up with my ignorance on this question if I did not fear that one of these opinions which conflicts with the firm belief to which we hold, might lead unwary minds astray. But until I know which of them I ought to choose, I profess that I confidently believe that the one which is true does not conflict with the strong and firmly founded faith according to which the Church of Christ believes that human babies, even newly-born ones, cannot be released from damnation except through the grace of Christ's name which he has granted to us through his sacraments.

## NOTES

1. Paulus Orosius was a priest from Spain where he was initially involved in the fight against the Priscillianist heresy. In 414 he moved to Africa where he became a friend of Augustine who sent him to the Holy Land to enlist Jerome's support in the fight against Pelagianism. He later undertook at Augustine's request the work for which he is best known, the Historia adversus Paganos.

2. Cf. 2 Tim. 2.21.

3. Orosius had written a work entitled Commonitorium de Errore Priscillianistarum et Origenistarum [CSEL 18.149-157], to which Augustine responded with his Ad Orosium contra Priscillianistas et Origenistas [P.L. 42.669-678].

4. Cf. 1 Tim. 6.16.

5. i.e. the Manichees. Cf. Aug. De Nat. Bon. cont. Manichaeos [CSEL 25], Contra Fortunatum and the De Continentia [CSEL 41].

6. The four elements of which the world was traditionally thought to be composed were earth, air, fire and water, but some writers mention earth, air, water and aether i.e. the pure fiery element above the air, e.g. Lucretius De Rerum Natura V.495-503.

7. Augustine is referring to what he wrote on free will in his De Libero Arbitrio [CCL 29.211-321], the De Genesi contra Manichaeos [P.L. 34], the De Vera Religione [CCL 32.187-260] and in the De Duabus Animabus [CSEL 25.1.pp. 51-80]. Indeed, so positively did Augustine speak of free will in these early works that Julian of Eclanum later said that he thought they showed that Augustine denied original sin.

8. Cf. Rom. 7.24.

9. i.e. the Pelagians.

10. Jer. Adv. Jovin. II.2 [P.L. 23.284].

11. Cf. Jer. Comm. in Jonam 3.5 [ed. P. Antin, Sources Chrétiennes 43, Paris 1956].

12. i.e. the three books De Libero Arbitrio [CCL 29] written during the period 388-395.

13. i.e. Jer. Ep. 126.1 [CSEL 56.143].

14. Cf. 1 Cor. 2.2.

15. Jer. Ep. 126.1 [CSEL 56.143].

16. Cf. Exod. 18.14-23.

17. Cf. Acts 10.25-48.

18. Cf. Gal. 2.11-21.

19. Cf. John 14.6, 1 John 5.7.

20. Cf. Gen. 2.2.

21. Cf. Gen. 1.26; on Augustine's solution to this problem Haren p. 50 speaks of 'his application of the Stoic theory of 'seminal reasons' to show that creation included, latently at least, all the causes of subsequent developments in the physical order. Although God rested from his labours on the seventh day, he had already established germinally in the perfected condition of his creation a dynamism sufficient to account for what followed.'

22. Sallust Jugurtha 2.3.

23. Jer. Adv. Ruf. III.28 [CCL 79.100].

24. Cf. Aug. Ep. 180.2 to Oceanus [CSEL 44.698].

25. Cf. Aug. dCD 22.22 [CCL 48.842-5] and Opus Imperf. cont. Julianum [P.L. 45.1049-1608 passim].

26. Cf. Lucretius De Rerum Natura III.760-4.

27. It is clear that Augustine regards this as an absurd idea, as did Lucretius who used a similar image in his argument against the immortality of the soul (III.776-780): 'Again, it is surely ridiculous to suppose that souls are standing by at the mating and birth of animals - a numberless number of immortals on the look-out for mortal bodies, jostling and squabbling to get in first.'

28. Aug. De Lib. Arb. III.68 [CCL 29.315].

29. Cf. Aug. de Pecc. Orig. 28 [CSEL 42.186-7].

30. Jer. Adv. Jov. II.2 [P.L. 23.284].

31. Jer. Comm. in Jonam 3.5.

32. Cf. Ps. 115.1 (116.10).

33. Cyprian Ep. 64.2-6 [CSEL 3.2.pp. 718-21].

34. Cf. John 3.5, a text which Augustine often refers to when discussing this question; see Schmid pp. 110-11.

35. Cf. Aug. De Gen. ad Litt. 10.6 [CSEL 28.1.pp. 302-3].

36. Cf. Aug. dCD 10.30, 12.21 [CCL 47.307-8, 48.376-9]; Augustine's scornful allusion to the theory of cosmic cycles is explained by Haren (p. 52) when he writes, '...against the Neoplatonist theory of cosmic cycles, developed from the Stoics, according to which universes succeed one another indefinitely and souls transmigrate, he offered a linear view of history.'

37. Cf. Luke 16.22.

AUGUSTINE EP. 167

The letter I wrote to you, Jerome, my honoured
brother in Christ, with my inquiry about the human soul
as to when, if new souls are still created individually
for each person who is born, they incur the debt of sin
which undoubtedly has to be cancelled by the sacrament
of Christ's grace even in the case of new-born babies -
extended to quite a sizeable volume,[1] so I decided
not to overload it by including any other question.
But the more urgent a question is, the less one can
afford to neglect it.  I therefore ask you and beg you
in the name of the Lord, to explain to me something
which I think will be of benefit to many; or if you
already possess some explanation written by you or
someone else, please  send it to me:   how should one
interpret the passage in the epistle of the apostle
James, 'For whoever keeps the whole law but fails in
one point has become guilty of all of it'? [James 2.10]
This is a question of such great importance that I
greatly regret not having written to you about it
earlier.

It is a question which concerns our behaviour in
the present life and the means by which we can attain
to life eternal; it is not concerned with investigating
the past which has sunk deep into oblivion, as was the
problem of the soul which I thought needed to be sorted
out.   There is a nice story which is relevant to this
point:   someone fell into a well where the water was
deep enough to hold him up and prevent him from
drowning but not such that he was choked by it and
unable to speak.   Another person came by and when he
saw him, he said sympathetically, 'How did you fall in

there?', to which the man answered, 'Please do not ask how I fell in but how you can get me out of here.' In the same way, since we confess and firmly believe in line with the Catholic faith that the soul of even a tiny baby must be delivered from the guilt of sin by the grace of Christ as from a well, it is enough to know how it can be saved, even if we never know how it incurred that evil. But I thought that we ought to make the investigation in case we might perhaps unthinkingly hold one of those opinions about the incarnation of the soul which, by denying that it is infected with this evil, contradicts the belief that the infant's soul definitely has to be released. I hold firmly to the belief that the infant's soul must be delivered from the guilt of sin and that there is no other means of release apart from the grace of God through Jesus Christ our Lord;[2] if we can also learn the cause and origin of this evil, we shall be readier and better prepared to resist those who foolishly engage in this discussion as if it were a petty dispute rather than a serious debate; but if we cannot, we should not be apathetic in our duty to show compassion just because the reason for the suffering is unknown. We are better protected against those who think they know what they do not, because we are not unaware of our own ignorance. There is a difference between what it is wrong not to know and what cannot be known or what it is not necessary to know or what is irrelevant for the life to which we aspire. But the passage in the epistle of James the apostle which I am now asking about is relevant to the way we live now and to the means by which we strive to please God so that we may live forever.

How then, I ask you, should one interpret the

words, 'Whoever keeps the whole law but fails in one point has become guilty of all'? [James 2.10] Is a thief guilty of murder, adultery and sacrilege? Or is even someone who says to a rich man, 'Sit here', while to a poor man he says, 'You stand over there' [James 2.3] guilty of such sins? If not, how does the person who fails in one point become guilty of all? Or is what I said about the rich and the poor man not included in those offences in respect of which if someone fails in one, he becomes guilty of all? But we should recall the source of this statement and its immediate context. The apostle writes, 'My brothers, show no partiality as you hold the faith of our Lord Jesus Christ, the Lord of glory. If a man with a gold ring and smart clothes enters your assembly and a poor man, shabbily dressed, also comes in, and you pay attention to the smartly dressed one and say to him, "Have a seat here, please", while you say to the poor man, "Stand over there or sit beneath my footstool", have you not judged within yourself and become judges of evil thoughts? Listen, my beloved brothers. Has not God chosen those who are poor in this world to be rich in the faith and heirs to the kingdom which God has promised to those who love him? But you have dishonoured the poor man,' [James 2.1-6] - no doubt referring to the one to whom it was said, 'You stand over there', although the man with the gold ring was told,'Have a seat here, please'. The apostle then goes on to give a broader treatment of the same statement, explaining it thus, 'Is it not the rich who use their power to oppress you and drag you into court? Do they not blaspheme that good name by which you are called? If you really fulfil the royal law of Scripture, 'You must love you neighbour as yourself', then you are doing well, but if you show partiality, you commit a sin and are convicted by the law as transgressors.' [James 2.6-9] Notice how he calls them transgressors of the law if they say to the rich man, 'Please sit here,' and to the poor man, 'Stand over there'. And then, in case they think that it is not a serious offence to transgress the law in this one point, he added, 'Whoever keeps the whole law but fails in one point, has become guilty of all, for he who said, "Do not commit adultery", also said, "Do not kill". If you do not kill but do commit adultery, you have become a transgressor of the law' [James 2.10-11], because he had already said, 'convicted by the law as transgressors'.

Since this is the case, it appears that unless someone can show me that the passage should be interpreted differently, because the person who said to the rich man, 'Sit here, please' but to the poor man, 'Stand over there', thereby accorded more respect to the one than the other, he will be judged to be an idolater, a blasphemer, an adulterer, a murderer, in short - for it would take too long to mention them all - he is found guilty of every sin: by failing on one point he has become guilty of all.

Conversely, the person who has one virtue would have them all, and he who does not have a particular one, would have none at all.[(3)] If this were so, then the statement under discussion would be proved true, but I do not wish to prove it, only to explain it, because in our eyes it has far greater authority in itself than the sayings of all the philosophers. But if what is said about the virtues and vices is true, it does not follow that because of this all sins are equal. I may be wrong, but if I remember rightly something of which I have only a dim recollection, this point about the inseparability of the virtues was accepted by all philosophers, who said that the same virtues are necessary for proper conduct in life. However, only the Stoics dared to argue for the equality of sins, thereby contradicting common human experience. With the support of Holy Scripture you have clearly refuted this foolish belief of theirs in your book against Jovinian[4] (who in his view of this question was a Stoic, although as far as his pursuit of pleasure and his repeated defence of it is concerned, he was an Epicurean.) From that elegant and remarkable discussion of yours it was abundantly clear that the idea that all sins are equal was not approved by Christian writers nor - and this is more important - by that Truth which spoke through them. With the Lord's help I shall try to explain as best I can how it can be the case that even if this is true of the virtues, we are not thereby forced to admit to the equality of all sins. If I manage to do this, you will approve; where my argument fails, you must supply what is necessary.

This is the argument used by those who believe that someone who has one virtue has them all and that if he lacks any one, he lacks them all: prudence cannot be cowardly or unjust or intemperate, for if it were any of these, it would not be prudence. However, if prudence must be brave and just and temperate to exist, then surely wherever it is found, it will be accompanied by the other virtues also. In the same way courage cannot be imprudent or intemperate or unjust and temperance must also be prudent, brave and just, while justice cannot exist unless it is prudent, brave and temperate. And so whenever one of them truly exists, the others are also to be found, but where the others are lacking, that one is not a true virtue, even though in some ways it seems to resemble one.

As you know, there are some faults which are clearly discernible as the opposites of certain virtues, as for example imprudence, which is the opposite of prudence; but there are others which are opposites only because they are faults, although they are deceptively similar to the virtue, as for example the relationship not between prudence and imprudence but between prudence and cunning. I now mean that kind of cunning which is more commonly understood and referred to in a bad sense, rather than in the sense used by our Scripture which often refers to cunning as something positive, as for example when it says, 'wise as serpents' [Matt. 10.16] or 'so that cunning may be given to the simple'. [Prov. 1.4] However, even among the pagans the most eloquent of Latin authors wrote, 'He did not lack the craft or cunning to be on his guard',[5] thereby giving 'cunning' a positive sense - although this use is very rare among them, but very common among Christian writers.

And then where temperance is concerned, prodigality is very clearly the opposite of thrift, while what is commonly called stinginess is obviously a vice but it bears a deceptive resemblance to thrift although it is not essentially the same. Similarly there is a clear difference between justice and injustice which makes one the opposite of the other, but the desire for revenge tends to resemble justice although it is a vice. Cowardice is obviously the opposite of courage; insensibility is by nature different from courage but its similarities deceive one into thinking they are the same. Constancy is a part of virtue; inconstancy is completely different and is undeniably its opposite, but obstinacy aspires to the name of constancy although it cannot assume it, for constancy is a virtue while obstinacy is a vice.

So as to avoid the necessity of repeating the same things, let me give an example which may explain everything. According to those who wrote about him and who were in a position to know, Catiline was able to bear cold, thirst and hunger; 'he could endure hunger, icy conditions and lack of sleep to an incredible degree',[6] and because of this, he seemed to himself and to his followers to be endowed with great fortitude. But this courage was not a prudent one for he used to choose bad things instead of good, neither was it temperate nor just, for it drove him to conspire against his country; and so it was not courage but insensibility assuming the name of courage so as to deceive the foolish. If it had been courage, it would have been a virtue, not a vice, but if it had been a virtue it would never have been deserted by the other virtues which are, as it were, its inseparable companions.

That is why when the question is raised about vices - whether they all exist simultaneously where there is one present or whether none of them exists if one of them is absent - it is difficult to prove, because each virtue tends to have vices opposed to it, both what is obviously its opposite and also something which has a specious resemblance to the virtue in question. It is easy to see that Catiline's courage did not really exist because it was not accompanied by the other virtues, but it is hard to be convinced that it was an unwillingness to face hardship, seeing that it manifested itself in the patient endurance of the most terrible difficulties of every kind, to a greater degree than one would think possible. Perhaps if one looks more closely, his hardihood will seem like an unwillingness to face hardship because he neglected the hard work involved in the pursuit of good, by which true courage is acquired. In fact, because those who are not fearful are bold and conversely those who lack boldness are timid (even though both characteristics are vices), whereas anyone who is truly brave neither ventures anything rashly nor fears anything without just cause, we are forced to admit that vices are more numerous than virtues.

That is why one vice is occasionally removed by another - for example, greed for money by desire for praise - and sometimes one gives way only to be replaced by several others, as when someone who was a drunkard strives to drink in moderation out of stinginess or ambition; and so vices can be replaced by other vices instead of virtues and that is why there are more of them. But where one virtue has entered, because it brings with it all the others, all the vices which were there undoubtedly give way; (of course, not all of them existed there but sometimes they are replaced by just as many vices, sometimes more are replaced by fewer or fewer by more.)

We must look into the problem carefully to see whether this is the case, for the assertion that anyone who has one virtue has them all, while he who lacks one, lacks them all has no divine authority. It has, it is true, seemed convincing to men who were very clever and learned and who had time to ponder this question, but they were still just men. I do not know how to put it: I am not denying that even a woman - not to mention a man from whom the word virtue is derived[7] - who remains faithful to her husband has

chastity, if she does so because of God's commandments
and promise and is faithful to him first of all; nor
would I say that chastity is not a real virtue or only
a minor one. The same is true of a husband who remains
faithful to his wife. Yet there are many such people,
none of whom I could say were without any fault, and
certainly their fault, whatever it is, comes from some
vice. But conjugal chastity in devout men and women is
undoubtedly a virtue - for it is not nothing nor is it
a vice - and yet it is not accompanied by all the
virtues; for if they were all there, there would be no
vice and if there were no vice, there would be no fault
whatsoever: but who is without fault? Who then is
without any vice, in other words without anything which
might spark a sin off or be the source of sin, when he
who leaned on the breast of the Lord cried out, 'If we
say that we have no sin, then we are deceiving
ourselves and truth is not in us'? [1 John 1.8]

There is no need to discuss this any longer for
your benefit, but I am saying all this for the sake of
others who might perhaps read it. Indeed you have
carefully proved this point, using the Holy Scriptures,
in that excellent work which you wrote against
Jovinian;(8) you also used this same epistle which was
the source of that passage for which we are now seeking
an explanation when you quoted the words, 'For we all
sin in many things.' [James 3.2] Although it was
Christ's apostle speaking he did not say, 'You sin,'
but 'We sin'; and although he says in this passage,
'Anyone who keeps the whole law but offends on one
point, becomes guilty of all' [James 2.10], he said
there that all, not just some, sin not in one point but
in many.

But God forbid that any believer should think that

so many thousands of Christ's servants have no virtue who honestly say that they are sinful, in case they should deceive themselves and there should be no truth in them, for wisdom is a great virtue. God said to man, 'Behold, reverence is wisdom.' [Job 28.28] Far be it from us to say that all these outstandingly faithful and reverent men of God do not have reverence which the Greeks call either eusebeia or, more accurately and meaningfully, theosebeia. But what is reverence if not worship of God? And why is he worshipped if not out of love? Love from a pure heart and a clear conscience and sincere faith[9] is a great and real virtue because it is also the end of the law. Love is rightly said to be strong as death[10] either because no one can overcome it any more than death or because in this life love continues right up to death - as the Lord says, 'Greater love has no man than this, that he lay down his own life for his friends' [John 15.13] - or rather because love tears the soul away from the carnal desires just as death tears it from the bodily senses. Knowledge is useful when it is subservient to love but without love, knowledge makes men conceited.[11] But in the measure that love fills the heart by edification, knowledge will find no room for conceit. Moreover Scripture has shown that knowledge is useful; after saying, 'Behold, reverence is wisdom,' it immediately adds, 'But to abstain from evil, that is knowledge.' [Job 28.28] Can we then not say that anyone who has this virtue has them all, since love is the fulfilment of the law?[12] Is it not true that the more love a man has, the more he is endowed with virtue, because it is itself a virtue, but the less he has, the less virtue is present and the less virtue he has, the more vice there is in him? And so where love is full and perfect, there will be no vice left.

The Stoics accordingly seem to me to be wrong in refusing to allow that a man who is making progress in wisdom has any wisdom at all, insisting as they do that he possesses wisdom only when he has reached perfection. It is not that they deny that he has advanced but they say that he is not wise at all unless he suddenly springs forth into the free air of wisdom, emerging out of the deep, so to speak. For just as it makes no difference to a man who is drowning whether the water above him is many fathoms deep or just a hand or finger's depth,[13] so they say that those who are striving towards wisdom are indeed making progress when they, as it were, rise up towards the air out of the depths of the whirlpool, but do not possess virtue and are not wise unless, by making progress, they have escaped from all foolishness, as if they were emerging from the water pressing down on them; once they have escaped they immediately possess all wisdom and there is no trace of foolishness which could be the source of any sin.

This comparison whereby foolishness is represented as water and wisdom as air, so that the soul, emerging into wisdom out of the foolishness in which it is drowning, is suddenly able to breathe, does not seem to me sufficiently pertinent to the authority of our Scriptures. A better comparison would be one where vice or foolishness was represented as darkness and virtue or wisdom as light - insofar as it is possible to compare physical things with intelligible ones. It is not as if the soul rises up into the air out of the water and as soon as it reaches the water's surface suddenly breathes in as much as it needs; it is more like someone moving from darkness towards the light who is gradually illuminated as he moves forward. But until this is fully accomplished we say that he is like someone emerging from a very deep cave: as he gets nearer to the exit, more light gradually reaches him and the light which reaches him undoubtedly comes from the light towards which he is moving, while what is still dark is part of that darkness out of which he is emerging. That is why no living person will be justified in the sight of God[14] and yet the just man lives by faith.[15] The saints are clothed in justice, one more so, another less, but no one lives here without sin, although some have more, some less: the best man is he who has the least.

But what am I doing? I seem to have forgotten to whom I am speaking. After setting out what I wished to learn from you, I am now acting like a teacher. But as the question of the equality of sins came up in my discussion, I decided to give an account of my view for you to scrutinise. Now at last I will bring it to a close, for even if it is true that the person who has one virtue possesses them all, while someone who does not possess a particular one has none, this does not imply that the sins are equal; although where no virtue exists, nothing is right, it can yet happen that one thing is more wrong or more perverse. However, I think it is more accurate and more in keeping with the sacred writings to say that the intentions of the soul are like the limbs of the body (although they cannot be seen in space, they are perceived by the emotions), one being more illuminated, another less, while another lacks light completely and is shrouded in darkness which inhibits it totally; in the same way each person is affected by the enlightenment of reverent love, more in one action, less in another and not at all in another, and so he can be said to have one virtue and not another and to have another more or less. For we can rightly say that there is greater love in one person than in another and that there is some in one and none in another, as far as love is concerned, for love is reverence; and with regard to one and the same man we can say that he has more chastity than patience and more today than yesterday, if he is making progress and that he does not yet possess continence but does have a good deal of compassion.

To give a brief, general summary of my idea of virtue, with regard to how to live properly; virtue is love by which one loves what one should love. This virtue is present to a greater degree in some, to a lesser degree in others and in others not at all, but the most perfect love which knows no increase is present in no one as long as he lives in this world; but as long as it can increase, the part that is less than it ought to be is undoubtedly such because of vice. On account of this vice there is no just man on earth who will do good and will not sin [Eccles. 7.21]; as a result of this vice, no living being will be justified in the sight of God [Ps. 142.2 (143.2)]; as a result of this vice, if we say that we have no sin, we are deceiving ourselves and there is no truth in us [1 John 1.8]; on account of it, however much progress we have made, we must still say, 'Forgive us our trespasses' [Matt. 6.12], even though all our words, deeds and thoughts have already been forgiven in baptism. Accordingly, he who sees rightly can see where, when and from where that perfection is to be hoped for, to which it is impossible to add anything. But if there were no commandments, a man would certainly have no way of looking at himself with certitude and seeing what he ought to avoid, and what he ought to be striving for, what he ought to rejoice in and what he should pray for. The commandments are therefore very useful, if only because free will is thereby granted the opportunity of doing greater honour to the grace of God.

If this is the case, how is it that someone who keeps the whole law but offends in one thing, becomes guilty of everything? [James 2.10] Could it perhaps be that because love is the fulfilment of the law,[16] by which God and our neighbour are loved, and because on the commandment to love hang the whole law and the prophets,[17] anyone who acts contrary to that love upon which everything depends deservedly becomes guilty of all? In fact, no one sins except by acting contrary to love because 'You must not commit adultery, you must not commit murder, you must not steal, you must not covet' and all the other commandments are summed up in this sentence, 'You must love your neighbour as yourself.' Love of neighbour does no wrong, and so love is the fulfilment of the law.[18] But no one loves his neighbour unless in loving God he does all he can to make his neighbour, whom he loves as himself, love God, too. If he does not love God, he loves neither himself nor his neighbour, and as a result, a person who keeps the whole law but offends in one thing becomes guilty of all, because he acts contrary to love on which the whole law depends. Accordingly he becomes guilty of everything by acting contrary to that upon which everything depends.

Why then can we not say that all sins are equal? Perhaps it is because anyone who commits a more serious offence is more guilty of contravening love, while he who commits a less serious one is less guilty. Both

are guilty of all, though the one who sins more
seriously or more often is more guilty than someone who
sins less seriously or less often. Of course, the more
serious the sin, the greater the guilt, and the less
serious the sin, the less heavy the guilt; and yet even
if a man offends in one thing only he is guilty of all
because he has acted contrary to the love upon which
all depends. If this is true, it explains what the man
of apostolic grace says - 'For we all offend in many
things' [James 3.2]; we do offend, but some do so more,
some less. The more seriously one sins, the less he
loves God and his neighbour and conversely, the less
one sins, the more he loves God and his neighbour; the
fuller he is of wickedness, the emptier he is of love,
and he is most perfect in love when there is no
weakness left in him.

If we apply this difference between sitting and
standing to ecclesiastical honours, one ought
definitely not, in my opinion, to think it a venial sin
to show partiality for one who professes faith in the
Lord Jesus Christ. Who could bear that a rich man
should be chosen to a place of honour in the Church,
while someone more learned and more holy was rejected
because he was poor? But if the apostle is talking
about everyday social intercourse, who does not sin in
this way - if indeed it is a sin - when he judges from
appearances that a rich man is a better man? This is
what the apostle seems to have meant when he said,
'Have you not judged within yourselves and become
corrupt judges?' [James 2.4]

And so the law of freedom is the law of love, of
which the apostle says, 'If then you fulfil the royal
law of the Scriptures, "You must love your neighbour as
yourself", you do well; but if you show partiality, you

are committing an offence and are convicted by the law
as transgressors.' [James 2.8-9] After this difficult
statement, about which I have said all that I think
needs saying, he mentions this same law of freedom when
he says, 'So speak and act as those who are to be
judged under the law of freedom.' [James 2.12] He
bears in mind what I mentioned[19] a little earlier,
namely that we all offend in many things, and so he
offers the Lord's daily remedy, as it were, for daily
wounds, even slight ones; he says, 'Judgement is
without mercy to one who has shown no mercy' [James
2.13]. That is why the Lord also said, 'Forgive and
you will be forgiven, give and it will be given to
you.' [Luke 6.37] Yet mercy triumphs over judgement.
[James 2.13] It does not say, 'Yet mercy overcomes
judgement,' for mercy is not an enemy of judgement, but
that it triumphs over it, because more people are
united by mercy, but only those who have shown mercy.
'Blessed are the merciful, for God will have mercy on
them.' [Matt. 5.7]

It is of course just that those who forgive should
be forgiven and that those who give should be given to,
for this balance between mercy and judgement is an
attribute of God. That is why one says to him, 'I will
sing of mercy and judgement to you, O Lord.' [Ps. 100.1
(101.1)] Anyone who is so confident of his
righteousness that he awaits judgement without calling
for mercy provokes a righteous wrath, in fear of which
the psalmist cried, 'Do not put your servant on trial'
[Ps. 142.2 (143.2)], and that is why God said to the
stubborn people,'Why do you wish to struggle against my
judgement?' [Jerem. 2.29] 'For when a just king sits
on the throne, who will boast that he has a pure heart?
Who will boast that he is clean from sin?' [Prov. 20.8-

9]    What  hope  is  there  unless  mercy  triumphs  over
judgement  [James  2.13]  -  but  only  for  those  who  have
shown  mercy  by  saying  sincerely,  'Forgive  us  as  we
forgive'  [Matt.  6.12],  and  by  giving  without
complaining?   For  God  loves  a  cheerful  giver  [2 Cor.
9.7].   Finally,  in  order  to  console  those  whom  this
statement  had  thoroughly  frightened,  following  on  from
that  passage  St. James  speaks  about  the  works  of  mercy
when  he  points  out  how  even  everyday  sins  without  which
man  cannot  live  in  this  world  are  expiated  by  daily
remedies;  without  them  man  who  when  he  offends  in  one
thing  becomes  guilty  of  all  and  who  offends  in  many
ways  because  in  many  things  we  all  offend  [James 3.2],
would  gradually  accumulate  a  large  amount  of  guilt  to
bring  before  the  tribunal  of  the  great  judge  and  would
not  find  that  mercy  which  he  himself  has  not  shown;
instead,  by  forgiving  and  by  giving  he  deserves  to  have
his  sins  forgiven  and  the  promised  reward  given  to  him.

I  have  spoken  at  length  and  perhaps  bored  you,  for
you  do  not  expect  to  learn  things  which  you  accept  and
which  you  are  accustomed  to  teach,  not  to  be  told.   If
there  is  anything  here  as  regards  the  subject  matter
(for  I  am  not  too  bothered  whether  it  has  been
eloquently  expressed)  -  if,  I  say,  there  is  anything
here  which  is  offensive  to  your  learning,  please  inform
me  in  your  reply  and  do  not  hesitate  to  correct  me.
Unfortunate  is  the  man  who  does  not  worthily  honour  the
important  and  holy  efforts  of  your  studies  and  give
thanks  for  them  to  the  Lord  our  God,  by  whose  gift  you
are  what  you  are.   And  so,  since  I  ought  to  be  willing
to  learn  from  anyone  what  it  is  unprofitable  for  me  not
to  know,  rather  than  keen  to  teach  others  what  I  know,
with  how  much  greater  reason  do  I  beg  for  this  favour
of  love  from  you  by  whose  teaching,  in  the  name  of  the

Lord and with his help, the literature of the Church in the Latin language has advanced more than was possible ever before! And I beg you for the Lord's sake, if you know of any better way of explaining this statement, 'Whoever keeps the whole law but offends in one thing becomes guilty of all' [James 2.10], be so kind as to communicate it to us.

## NOTES

1. i.e. Aug. Ep. 166.

2. Cf. Rom. 7.24.

3. Cicero in his De Officiis (II.10.35) wrote, 'It is generally agreed by all philosophers and I myself have often argued that he who has one virtue has them all' ; cf. Diog. Laert. VII.125.

4. Jer. Adv. Jov. I.1 [P.L. 23.211], II.21 [315] and II.36 [333-4].

5. i.e. Sallust, in his Catilina 26.2.

6. ibid. 5.3.

7. Varro in his De Lingua Latina (V.73) wrote that 'Virtue/valour is from virilitas' (manhood).

8. Jer. Adv. Jov. II.2 [P.L. 23.284].

9. Cf. 1 Tim. 1.5.

10. Cant. 8.6.

11. Cf. 1 Cor. 8.1.

12. Cf. Rom. 13.10.

13. For the metaphor of drowning see Sandbach p. 45, 'The Stoics maintained that there were no grades of

badness: a man, said Chrysippus, who is a cubit below the surface drowns as much as one who is five hundred fathoms down.'

14. Cf. Ps. 142.2 (143.2).

15. Cf. Eccles. 7.21.

16. Cf. Rom. 13.10.

17. Cf. Matt. 22.40.

18. Cf. Rom. 13.9-10.

19. The text here is problematic: if we accept the reading of Goldbacher [CSEL 44.606] (dixerit) Augustine seems to be implying that the passage he now quotes, from James 3.2, comes before the passages from James 2 to which he has been referring. Perhaps we should read dixerim and explain it as Augustine referring to the verse James 3.2 which he mentioned earlier in this letter.

JEROME EP. 134

I was glad to welcome the priest Orosius,[1] both because of his own merits and because you asked me to do so. He is an honourable man who stands as a brother to me and a son to you. But we are going through a very difficult time, and it has seemed better for me to remain silent than to speak; as a result our studies have come to a halt and, in Appius' words,[2] my speech is but a snarl. I have been unable to reply for the moment to the two long letters[3] which you dedicated to me, both very learned works, glittering with every brilliant rhetorical effect; it is not that I thought anything in them needed to be criticised but, according to the blessed apostle, each man should be free to hold his own opinion,[4] one in this way, another in that. In fact, everything that could be said, drawn from the springs of Holy Scripture by a lofty mind, has been mentioned and discussed by you. But I beg you to allow me for the moment just to praise your genius; for you and I carry on discussions with one another for the sake of learning, but if those who are our rivals, especially the heretics, see that we hold conflicting opinions, they will falsely conclude that this is due to ill-feeling between us. I have decided to love you, welcome you, honour you, admire you and to defend your words as if they were my own - in fact, in the dialogue which I recently published I mentioned you as was proper.[5] Let us make a greater effort to eradicate that most dangerous heresy from the churches; it always pretends to repentance so that it may have an opportunity of teaching in the churches, fearing that if it comes out into the open, it would be driven out and die.

Your holy and venerable daughters Eustochium and Paula[6] lead lives worthy of their rank as well as of your encouragement; they greet you specifically, as do all the brothers who try along with me to serve the Lord, our saviour. Last year we sent the holy priest Firmus to Ravenna on business for them, and then on to Africa and Sicily; I think he must still be staying somewhere in Africa. I ask you to greet those holy men who are your close companions. I have also sent a letter of mine to the holy priest Firmus; if it should reach you, please be so kind as to forward it to him. May Christ our Lord keep you safe and mindful of me, my lord, truly holy and most blessed bishop.

P.S. We are experiencing a great shortage of Latin speaking scribes in this province and that is why I am unable to obey your orders, especially regarding the edition of the Septuagint which has been marked with asterisks and obelisks; also, I have lost a large part of my earlier work because of someone's dishonesty.[7]

## NOTES

1. See Aug. Ep. 166 n. 1 above.

2. Cf. Sallust *Historia* II.37, Jer. Ep. 119.1.

3. i.e. Aug. Ep. 166 and Ep. 167.

4. Cf. Rom. 14.5.

5. Jer. Dial. adv. Pelag. III.19 [P.L. 23.588-90].

6. Eustochium was the daughter of the elder Paula, while the Paula referred to here is Eustochium's niece, the elder Paula's granddaughter; it was with regard to her education that Jerome wrote his Ep. 107 to her mother Laeta and it was she who later took over the running of the monastery founded by her grandmother.

7. On Jerome's translation of the Septuagint into Latin, see the Introduction p. 8.

JEROME EP. 141

I have always revered you with the honour which is proper and I have loved the Lord our saviour dwelling in you, but now, if it is possible, I add something more to the pile and fill what is already full; as a result I cannot allow a single hour to pass without mention of your name, for you have stood firm in your ardent faith against the blasts of the storm and have preferred, as far as you were able, to be delivered from Sodom on your own rather than to remain with those who are dying: you know what I am referring to. Well done! You are famous throughout the world; the Catholics revere you and honour you as the second founder of their ancient faith, while (and this is a sign of greater honour) all the heretics hate you and persecute me, too, with equal hatred; they hope to kill merely by wishing those whom they cannot kill by the sword.[1] May the mercy of Christ our Lord keep you safe and mindful of me, reverent lord and most blessed bishop.

NOTES

1. Cf. Jer. Epp. 135-8 [CSEL 56.263-6]; Aug. De Gest. Pelag. 66 [CSEL 42.121-2].

JEROME EP. 142

Many people[1] are lame on both feet and go about with bent heads even though their necks are not broken, preserving an attachment to their former error although they do not have the same freedom to preach. The holy brothers who are with me, and your holy and venerable daughters[2] especially greet you humbly. I beg you to greet in my name your brothers, my lord Alypius and my lord Evodius.[3] Jerusalem is held captive by Nebuchadnezzar and refuses to listen to the advice of Jeremiah; instead it longs for Egypt, to die at Taphnes and there perish in everlasting slavery.[4]

## NOTES

1. i.e. Pelagians.

2. i.e. Paula the younger and Eustochium.

3. Evodius, bishop of Uzalis in N. Africa, was born at Thagaste like Augustine but it seems that they only became friends when they were both in Milan; cf. Aug. Conf. IX.8.17, IX.12.31.

4. Jerome is intentionally enigmatic here; it is possible that Nebuchadnezzar refers to John of Jerusalem. For Nebuchadnezzar, Egypt and Taphnes, cf. Jerem. 43 in which Jeremiah and the people of Judah refuse to listen to God when he warns them not to go into Egypt after Jerusalem has been taken captive by Nebuchadnezzar, the king of Babylon.

JEROME EP. 143

Jerome sends greetings in Christ to the bishops Alypius
and Augustine, his truly holy lords, worthy of respect
and all affection.

The holy priest Innocent who is the bearer of this
letter, did not deliver what I had written to you last
year as he did not think he would be returning to
Africa. Nevertheless we thank God that things turned
out in such a way that your letters got the better of
my silence. Every opportunity of writing to you is
most welcome to me, and I call God to witness that if
it were possible, I would take the wings of a dove and
fly into your embrace.[1] This has in fact always been
the case because of your virtues, but it is now
especially true because the heresy of Caelestius[2] has
been silenced at your instigation and with your
cooperation. This heresy has so infected the hearts of
many that when they perceive that they are defeated and
condemned, they still do not reject the poison from
their minds: the only thing they can do now is to hate
us whom they believe to be responsible for their loss
of freedom to teach their heresy.

You ask whether I have written a reply against the
books of Annianus,[3] the false deacon of Celenderis,
who feasts himself grossly so as to supply empty words
to another's blasphemy:[4] you should know that I
received those books copied on small sheets of paper
not long ago from our holy brother, the priest
Eusebius,[5] and since then I have been so upset by the
worsening illness and by the death of our holy and
revered daughter Eustochium[6] that I almost thought I

should throw them away. That man remains stuck in the same bog and says nothing new apart from a few tinkling words which sound as if they have been begged from somewhere. I have however achieved something important: when he tries to reply to my letter,[7] he betrays himself more openly and reveals his blasphemies to all. For in this work he professes everything he denies having said at that wretched synod at Diospolis,[8] and it is no great task to answer his foolish nonsense. But if the Lord grants me life, and if I have enough copyists, I will reply in what will be a few nights' work, not in order to confute a heresy which is dead, but to prove his ignorance and blasphemy by means of my own arguments. You would do this better than me; then I would not be forced to praise my own works in opposing the heretic.

The holy children whom we share, Albina, Pinianus and Melania,[9] send their warmest greetings. I have given this brief letter to the holy priest Innocent for him to deliver from holy Bethlehem. Your granddaughter Paula[10] begs you in her grief to remember her and sends you her very best wishes. May the mercy of Christ our Lord keep you safe and mindful of me, my truly holy lords and fathers, revered and loved by all.

## NOTES

1. Cf. Ps. 54.7 (55.6).

2. Caelestius was a heretic closely associated with Pelagius; he went so far as to deny that baptism is for the remission of sins and even denied original sin. He was condemned at the council of Carthage in 412 but he

later resurfaced at Rome and for a time enjoyed the support of Pope Zosimus.

3. The writings of Annianus are lost and little is known of him but it seems that he was the first to translate several of the homilies of John Chrysostom into Latin (cf. Schmid p. 127).

4. i.e. Pelagius.

5. On Eusebius of Cremona, who had been a friend of Jerome since at least 393, see Cavallera *passim*.

6. Eustochium died in about 419 at about the age of 49.

7. i.e. Jer. Dial. adv. Pelag. [P.L. 23.495-590].

8. The synod at Diospolis (Lydda) took place at the end of 415. Pelagius managed to reassure the bishops as to his doctrinal position while apparently accepting the error of the views for which Caelestius had been condemned. Cf. Pelagius, Ep. ad Innocent. Papam [P.L. 48.610].

9. Albina was the daughter of the elder Melania, Rufinus' friend and Melania was her granddaughter who, together with her husband Pinianus, had left Rome in 408, fleeing before the Goths, and came by way of Africa to settle in the Holy Land, entering monasteries at Bethlehem.

10. For Paula, see Jer. Ep. 142 n. 2 above.

## APPENDIX:

Ep. 74 AUGUSTINE TO PRAESIDIUS[1]


While I was with you I asked you , and I urge you now, too, not to fail to send my letter[2] to our holy brother and your fellow priest, Jerome. As you are aware of the obligation you have to write to him on my behalf, I have also sent you copies both of my letter to him and of his to me; when you have read them in the light of your holy wisdom, you will easily perceive both my moderation, which I thought I ought to preserve, and his irritation, which I was quite justified in fearing. If I have written anything which I should not have or have not written it in the right way, then do not write to him about me but rather write to me, in brotherly love, so that I may be corrected and may ask him to forgive me if I admit my own fault.


### NOTES

1. Praesidius is mentioned as a deacon in Jer. Ep. 103.1 and as a priest in Aug. Ep. 74, while from Aug. Ep. 176 it would seem that he later became a bishop for his name appears in a list of bishops attending the Council of Milevis in 416.

2. i.e. Aug. Ep. 73.

Ep. 126 JEROME TO MARCELLINUS AND ANAPSYCHIA

Jerome sends greetings in Christ to Marcellinus and Anapsychia,[1] my truly holy lord and lady and also children whom I honour in all love and friendship.

The letter you sent me from Africa has at last reached me. I do not regret my rudeness in forcing my letters on you so often despite your refusal to answer, for I hoped I would deserve a reply and learn that you were well, not from someone else but preferably from your own words. I remember your little query - or rather that question which is of the greatest moment to the Church - about the nature of the soul: you asked whether the soul has fallen from heaven, as the philosopher Pythagoras believed, as well as Origen and all the Platonists, or whether it is an offshoot of the divine being, as the Stoics, the Manichaean heretics and the Priscillianists in Spain suppose, or whether, once they have been created long ago, God stores the souls in a sort of treasury, a belief of which some churchmen are foolishly persuaded. It has also been suggested tht souls are made each day by God and are sent into bodies, according to the words of the Gospel, 'My Father is working even now and so am I' [John 5.17], or that, as Tertullian, Apollinaris and most western Christians affirm, souls come into being through propagation, in such a way that one soul is born from another just as one body is born from another and that it has the same nature as brute animals. As to my opinion, I recall that long ago in my works against Rufinus I wrote something to counter his argument in that book he addressed to Anastasius,[2] the Roman bishop of sacred memory; in that work he tried to cheat the naivety of his readers by means of a deceitful and cunning, no, rather a foolish confession, but really he was fooling his own faith or rather his lack of it. I believe your holy relative Oceanus possesses a copy of these books. It is a long time since Rufinus' books which poured out calumnies against me were widely published. Of course you do have with you in Africa that holy and learned man, bishop Augustine; he can teach you by his living voice, so to speak, and explain his view, or rather my view by means of his own.

I have long wished to undertake a commentary on Ezechiel[3] and to fulfil for my eager readers an oft-repeated promise, but when I began to dictate, my mind was thrown into confusion by the devastation of the western provinces and especially of Rome itself; as a result I hardly knew my own name (to use the common proverb) and for a long time I have kept silent, knowing that it is a time for tears. But this year when I have managed to write three books of my commentary, the sudden onslaught of the barbarians (whom your beloved Virgil refers to as the far-flung Barcaei, while Holy Scripture says of Ismael, 'He will live against the face of all his brothers')[4] has spread across Egypt, Palestine, Phoenicia and Syria, carrying everything before it like a torrent, so that we have hardly been able to escape them by Christ's mercy. But if, according to that distinguished orator, the laws are silent in times of war,[5] how much more true is this of the study of Scripture which requires a large number of books as well as silence and hard work on the part of the copyists, and in particular, peace

and quiet for those dictating!    I have sent two books
to my daughter Fabiola[6] and you can borrow copies of
them from her, if you wish.    Lack of time prevents me
from transcribing the others.    When you have read them
and seen the entrance hall, as it were, you can easily
imagine what the house will look like.    But I believe
in God's mercy which has helped us in the difficult
beginning of the above-mentioned work[7] and I trust
that he will give his support to it near the end of the
prophet's writings where the wars of Gog and Magog are
recounted and at the very end where the building of
that most holy and intricate temple, its variety and
measurements are described.

Our holy brother Oceanus,[8] to whom you wish to be
commended, is such a great man and so learned in the
law of the Lord that he can instruct you without my
asking him and he can explain my opinion on all the
problems of Scripture according to the measure of my
talent.    May Christ our God, the omnipotent, keep you
hale and hearty to a great age, my truly holy lords.


NOTES


1. Flavius Marcellinus was a man in high office in the
Roman administration; he had come to Africa in 411 when
appointed by Honorius to preside over an investigation
into the disputes between the Catholics and the
Donatists.    He became an intimate friend of Augustine
who addressed the first two books of the De Civitate
Dei to this man.    He was later imprisoned and executed
and is regarded as a martyr by the Catholic Church. It
is unclear who Anapsychia was, but it is more probable
that this person was Marcellinus' wife than that it was
a (male) friend or colleague of Marcellinus; the fact
that Jerome addresses them together as domini and filii
does not imply that they were both men as this was a

common form of address for a husband and wife (cf. Aug. Ep. 45 to Paulinus and Therasia) or in the case of the addressees being a group of men and women (e.g. Aug. Ep. 124 to Albina, Pinianus and Melania, the three members of the same family whom Jerome refers to in his Ep. 143).

2. For Rufinus' Apology to Anastasius which Jerome regarded as part of Rufinus' attack on him, see CCL 20.19-28.

3. Jer. Comm. in Ezechiel, in fourteen books, was composed with difficulty during the years 410-414. (See CCL 75).

4. Virg. Aen. 4.42; Gen. 16.12.

5. Cicero Pro Milone IV.11.

6. The Fabiola to whom Jerome sent part of his commentary on Ezechiel is not to be confused with the lady of the same name who was a close friend and admirer of Jerome since his stay in Rome but who had died in 399 (cf. Jerome's letter to Oceanus on her death). Little is known of this woman except that she was also a correspondent of Augustine (cf. Aug. Ep. 267).

7. i.e. the commentary on Ezechiel.

8. Oceanus was possibly a senator who was a friend both of Jerome and of Augustine and apparently a relative of the elder Fabiola. In Augustine's Ep. 76 he is referred to as Marcellinus' spiritual father and Augustine later wrote a letter to him (Ep. 180) on the subject of the topics which he had discussed in his Ep. 82 and Ep. 166 to Jerome.

# INDEX

# INDEX OF BIBLICAL REFERENCES